CATCH
a Falling
Reader

Second Edition

Dedicated to Dr. Marie M. Clay, one of my greatest heroes in the field. May her memory and her work be eternal.

CATCH
a Falling Reader

Second Edition

Connie R. Hebert

CORWIN PRESS
A SAGE Company
Thousand Oaks, CA 91320

For information:

Corwin Press
A SAGE Company
2455 Teller Road
Thousand Oaks, California 91320
www.corwinpress.com

SAGE Ltd.
1 Oliver's Yard
55 City Road
London EC1Y 1SP
United Kingdom

SAGE India Pvt. Ltd.
B 1/I 1 Mohan Cooperative
Industrial Area
Mathura Road, New Delhi 110 044
India

SAGE Asia-Pacific Pte. Ltd.
33 Pekin Street #02-01
Far East Square
Singapore 048763

Printed in the United States of America.

Library of Congress Cataloging-in-Publication Data

Hebert, Connie R.
Catch a falling reader/Connie R. Hebert.
    p. cm.
Includes bibliographical references and index.
ISBN 978-1-4129-5605-5 (cloth)
ISBN 978-1-4129-5606-2 (pbk.)
    1. Reading (Primary) 2. Education, Primary—Activity programs. I. Title.

LB1525.H43 2008
372.4—dc22   2007029948

This book is printed on acid-free paper.

10   11   10   9   8   7   6   5   4   3   2

Acquisitions Editor:	Stacy Wagner
Managing Editor:	Jessica Allan
Editorial Assistant:	Joanna Coelho
Production Editor:	Eric Garner
Copy Editor:	Barbara Coster
Typesetter:	C&M Digitals (P) Ltd.
Proofreader:	Charlotte J. Waisner
Indexer:	Ellen Slavitz
Cover Designer:	Scott Van Atta
Graphic Designer:	Lisa Miller

Contents

Foreword

C atch a Falling Reader is a heartfelt expression of the author's passion for motivating teachers to impact the lives of all children. Nationally acclaimed literacy consultant Dr. Connie Hebert shares her training and experiences that make her an outstanding practitioner and eminently qualified to lead the charge on literacy. In this concise and straightforward resource, Dr. Hebert gives educators, administrators, and parents a gift: more than 40 "timeless" instructional literacy strategies that can be used in every classroom to help every struggling reader. She succeeds in providing practitioners with numerous opportunities to practice and reflect on instructional reading methods when catching and teaching "falling readers."

Teacher turnover in schools is almost 50% in the first three years. Training and support is fundamental for ongoing professional development, which in turn directly impacts student achievement. This unique book provides step-by-step strategies for teachers that will improve instruction. It breaks down a complex skill set of reading components into manageable parts, serves as an easy-to-follow guide for classroom teachers, and provides tangible strategies for those who work specifically with struggling readers.

As Louis Rubin states in his book *Artistry in Teaching,* "A passion for enlightening young minds is the driving force behind master teachers." After years of classroom teaching and consultation, Dr. Hebert has authored a book that is especially beneficial to new teachers, reading specialists, paraprofessional assistants, and mentors, whose support and guidance serve as a basis of professional development. School administrators too will find a host of strategies that may be used when coaching and supervising elementary teachers as they develop and refine their craft.

Expectations are often lowered for the struggling student. Furthermore, the majority of these students are being held to the same standard of proficiency on Grades 3–8 assessments and graduation criteria across the country. As educators, have we become part of the problem? Most college programs require a minimum number of courses for reading instruction, yet the primary responsibility for the teachers is to teach all children to read. Schools cannot rely solely on postsecondary education to teach their staff. We must provide ongoing training for teachers. If children are not taught to read at the elementary level, the failure gets carried into middle school and high school.

The instructional challenge for teachers is to differentiate and meet the needs of diverse learners in today's classroom. Struggling readers have not developed the same set of mental processes and skills needed to apply and utilize skills for decoding, comprehension, and writing. These students have developed coping mechanisms to deal with their reading, often exhibiting frustration, detachment, and lack of motivation.

All three sections of *Catch a Falling Reader* provide strategies that are sure to heighten the daily delivery of reading, writing, and thinking instruction through research-based best practices. Part I, Motivation Works Wonders, stresses the importance of the teacher's ability to motivate, engage, and "catch" falling readers in a variety of ways. Part II, Instructional Strategies Produce Results, addresses common habits of struggling readers, implementation of timeless best practices, assessment to drive instruction, and creative instructional techniques. Part III, Reflection Promotes Action, emphasizes the importance of teacher reflection in becoming a master teacher of struggling readers.

Reflect, observe, and teach is the mantra of good teachers. Our job is to assist students in becoming independent, risk-taking, confident learners who can problem solve, comprehend, and respond to higher-order thinking questions. That is the goal of all teachers. Proficient teachers keep their eyes on this goal, believing they can make a difference through passion, dedication, effort, compassion, and rigorous teaching methods.

Dr. Hebert has been recognized as a teacher of teachers, and her work has transformed literacy instruction across the country. She certainly impacted the delivery of reading instruction in our school district. Through modeling with students and training and coaching teachers, she motivated even the most discouraged teachers to approach the teaching of reading with new hope and higher expectations.

School personnel have an incredible challenge in their attempts to meet the needs of all students. In light of the No Child Left Behind federal legislation, educators are required to balance daily instructional needs with the needs of families and children. All children have the right to read, and this book shows educators how they can help children achieve this critical skill. The development of great teachers takes training, practice, and reflection. Dr. Hebert inspires and motivates learners of all ages with her fearless commitment and belief that we can "Catch Them ALL."

—Diane Albano, EdD
Assistant Superintendent for Instruction
Selkirk, NY

Acknowledgments

G reat teachers continually strive to become better teachers as they guide children toward becoming independent readers, writers, and thinkers. I have been blessed with many "great" teachers in my life; among them, my students, who gave me the opportunity to learn, grow, and practice. My most remarkable teachers, young and old, are embedded in this "timeless" book, and I am indebted to each one of them for their inspiration, expertise, and courage: Lizzie, Luke, Emily, Gabby, Glenn, Laurel Dickey, Dr. Diane Lowe, Dr. Diane Albano, Alfredo, Peter Thomsen, my three children (Tiffany, Gabriel, Daniel), my husband and best friend, David, my parents, Michael and Artemis Romell, my grandmother, Anna Tatamanis, and the greatest teacher of them all, Jesus Christ.

Many thanks to Stacy Wagner, Jessica Allan, Eric Garner, Barbara Coster, and all the good people of Corwin Press/SAGE for believing in the power of this book. Together, we can "Catch Them ALL." Special thanks to Lorraine Maslow, my editor and typist, and to Skip Makely at Authorhouse, who gave the book its first wings.

Corwin Press wishes to thank the following peer reviewers for their editorial insight and guidance:

Lettie K. Albright, PhD
Associate Professor of Reading
Texas Woman's University
Denton, TX

Susan Bolte
Principal
Providence Elementary
Aubrey, TX

Karla Bronzynski
First Grade Teacher
Eldora-New Providence
Eldora, IA

Denise L. Carlson
Curriculum Consultant
Heartland Area Education Agency
Johnston, IA

Tracy Carbone
Reading Recovery Teacher
Indian Trail Elementary
Indian Trail, NC

J. Richard Gentry, PhD
Author, Researcher, Educational Consultant
Fort Lauderdale, FL

Laura Linde
Literacy Coach/DIBELS Coordinator
Hoover Elementary School
North Mankato, MN

Ganna Maymind
First Grade Teacher
Asher Holmes Elementary School
Morganville, NJ

Harriet Mills
Literacy Coach/EIP Teacher
Wadsworth Elementary
Decatur, GA

Gail Underwood
Second Grade Teacher
Grant Elementary School
Columbia, MO

About the Author

Connie R. Hebert, EdD, is a nationally acclaimed teacher of teachers, reading specialist, and motivational speaker. Her company, EINNOC Educational Enterprises, LLC, is dedicated to motivating, teaching, and inspiring educators around the world. She received a doctorate in educational leadership, a master's degree in reading from the College of William & Mary, and a Reading Recovery certification from Lesley University. Experience in the field includes Director of Reading (K–12), elementary teacher (seven school districts), reading specialist (K–6), gifted and talented teacher, elementary music teacher, and Reading Recovery teacher (three school districts). She is the author of *Catch a Falling Reader* (2005) and *Catch a Falling Teacher* (2006). She served nine years as a senior national consultant for SDE (Staff Development for Educators) and three years as a literacy consultant for Macmillan/McGraw-Hill's Treasures program. She has been a national faculty instructor for Lesley University and served as a language arts instructor in four Massachusetts state colleges. She has spoken for teachers in 47 states and for many national, state, and European state reading conferences. She can be reached at www.conniehebert.com or dr.conniehebert@comcast.net.

Introduction

We all know that there are many different ways to catch something. Sometimes we stand in one place and hold our arms up because we expect something to fall. Other times we turn quickly and catch something that is thrown at us, just in time. We might even dive for an object that appears to be falling rapidly, or we simply jump up and try to make the catch. Even though we try to make a catch, there are times when we may miss it. In these instances, we usually bend down and pick it up anyway. What I am actually describing is what many of us have experienced with children who struggle to learn to read. The main point is that we must not give up in our attempts to catch these kids. They must be caught, taught, and let go!

Catch a Falling Reader is a "timeless" resource for educators because it will still be relevant 20 years from now, no matter which way the educational pendulum swings. It was written for the purpose of confirming, instructing, supporting, and inspiring those who teach children to read. The foundation for this work stems from research-based strategies along with decades of observation and instruction with children of all ages, training from some of the best teachers and researchers in the world, and years of teaching teachers around the globe. Who is this book mainly for? It is most useful for teachers and reading specialists who teach children who struggle with reading and writing, no matter what grade they may be in.

The ultimate challenge comes from knowing *how* to recognize when a child is falling, *when* to make the catch, and *what* to do about it. What can this book do for those who seek to catch a falling reader?

1. Offer ideas in a format that is easy to read and understand. This is not a textbook. Ideas and suggestions have been gathered from actual experiences in the field, in combination with research-based findings.

2. Create a conscious awareness of common behaviors in young readers that often become habits.

3. Recommend research-based strategies and methods for preventing falling readers from continuing to fall.

4. Provide opportunities for readers to confirm, reflect, and enhance their current knowledge of how to help falling readers.

The best way to read this book is simply to make it a daily practice—reading, reflecting, and perhaps trying one or two strategies each week. You may also want to allow the book to serve as a springboard for teacher book club discussions and debates. *Catch a Falling Reader* is divided into three specific sections: motivation, instructional strategies, and reflection. These three areas were selected as a way of organizing the information into manageable chunks. Segments within each section do not need to be read in any particular order. Teachers of students with special needs as well as those learning a second language will benefit from many of the strategies offered, but with modification and differentiation. Reflection is a key to understanding the craft of teaching falling readers. As educators and parents, we all struggle to find enough time to actually "think" about our teaching practices and theories. This book was created with that reality in mind.

For the purposes of this book, a *falling reader* refers to any child who is not where he or she needs to be in order to feel successful with text levels and literacy challenges that are expected at any given grade level. Falling readers can be spotted if we, as teachers and parents, become acutely aware of red flags that often present themselves in the early stages of reading development. The tricky part is that red flags come in a host of different shapes and sizes. These flags often appear during the preschool and kindergarten years but don't always manifest themselves fully until Grade 1.

Some early warning signs among falling readers appear to be more common than others. Teachers and reading specialists who are aware of these behaviors will want to begin where the learner is and build on strengths in order to move the reader forward. This awareness leads us to search for contributing factors and ultimately a plan of action.

Listed below are the most common early warning signs that we should watch for while teaching and guiding young learners. They include, but are not limited to the following:

(*Note:* Early warning signs do not necessarily appear in this order for any given child.)

- Delayed speech and language skills
- Frequent ear infections during toddler and preschool years
- Word retrieval difficulties (trouble "finding" words when retelling, explaining, or describing things, stories, or events)
- Phonemic awareness issues (limited letter and sound knowledge)
- Alphabet identification inaccuracy or inconsistency
- Rhyming difficulties or confusions
- Limited prior knowledge, vocabulary, and background experiences
- Directionality issues (right-left, top-bottom, front-back, before-after)
- Limited book-handling skills
- Unusually short attention span when listening to books or coloring
- Little or no interest in books
- Little or no attempts at attending to print (doesn't understand that print carries meaning)
- Little or no memory for patterned text
- Limited writing vocabulary
- Little or no instant recognition of basic sight words ("yes," "no," "Mom," "a," "I")
- Blinking, yawning, frowning, wiggling, or other unusual behaviors during reading group lessons or while reading to someone
- Looking up and waiting for someone to tell them the word
- Sounding out and/or distorting every letter on new and difficult words
- Guessing at words (based mainly on the first letter or letters)

- Skipping words often as a way of avoiding new and/or difficult words
- Frequently asking, "What's that word?"
- Reading painfully (word-by-word reading with little or no blending of words into phrases)

The power to catch a struggling child is at the heart of this book. Imagine the academic and social opportunities that exist for kids who are caught before frustration, bad habits, and low self-esteem take root and grow. Good teachers, therefore, continually strive to become better teachers by searching for what works and doesn't work in the struggle to help children become independent readers, writers, and thinkers. This continual pursuit requires commitment, patience, flexibility, skill, and sheer will!

It is my sincere hope that this book will inspire each reader to catch every falling student along the universal path to literacy. I firmly believe that, when we teach children how to fly as readers and writers, we save them. We must strive to prevent each and every falling reader from a lifetime of frustration, low self-esteem, anxiety, and disappointment. For, if we are not about catching kids and teaching them how to fly, then what are we really about?

Catch a falling reader and never let one get away!

Part I

Motivation Works Wonders

M otivation is the key to engaging students in "teachable moments." These precious moments provide windows of opportunity for teachers to actively involve students in the teaching and learning cycle. This section offers a variety of ways to motivate falling readers, including the use of voice, pace, body language, and eye contact. Although reading and discussing these ideas are necessary, it is only through practice that we actually launch ideas into action. Once we become aware of different motivational techniques, we can put them into action and make adjustments for meeting the diverse needs of the students in our care. If we truly want to become masters at motivating children, we must watch and learn from masterful teachers. This section is only a beginning.

Catch a Falling Reader by . . . *Standing on a Chair and Clapping*
Catch a Falling Reader by . . . *Using the Power of the Book Choice*
Catch a Falling Reader by . . . *Adjusting Our Tone of Voice . . . Frequently*
Catch a Falling Reader by . . . *Making Eye Contact at Teachable Moments*
Catch a Falling Reader by . . . *Adjusting the Pace of Each Lesson*
Catch a Falling Reader by . . . *Using Different Forms of Feedback*
Catch a Falling Reader by . . . *Setting a Purpose for Reading*

Catch a Falling Reader by . . . *Stimulating and Motivating Children With Puppets*

Catch a Falling Reader by . . . *Using Physical Actions to Help Kids Remember*

Catch a Falling Reader by . . . *Creating Bridges for Kids*

1

Catch a
Falling Reader by . . .

Standing on a
Chair and Clapping

If you would lift me up you must be on higher ground.

—Ralph Waldo Emerson

Have you ever glanced at the face of a struggling child when he or she looks at you with wonder and hope? I have! This proud, joyful look is witnessed each and every time I stand on a chair and clap for kids. It's as if the child is thinking, "Wow, I did that right. I think I'll do it again!" We all want to "do good," and we long to be applauded when we do. This most basic human need is important and necessary if we truly want to catch kids and help them fly to new heights.

It is important that we differentiate feedback for different kids. Some respond well to positive verbal comments such as, "I like the way you made that first sound when you were figuring out that word." Others thrive with a pat on the back or a smile (if they're sitting still long enough to notice either one). Still, there are those who prefer a written comment, sticker, or reward chart.

Feedback is an interesting concept, one that should not be taken lightly by teachers and parents. In fact, we all benefit from feedback, but the challenge comes in knowing how and when to offer it.

As we reflect on the feedback issue, let's consider five basic questions for a moment:

- **Who** are falling kids? Many are children who have not had the advantages that others have had. Some are children who have had many advantages, but they find learning difficult. All of them need constant, daily feedback in order to engage them to take risks and apply skills to new learning tasks.
- **What** do these kids want? They want to feel successful, each and every day!
- **Where** are they when they need feedback the most? They are usually involved in learning tasks that are difficult, challenging, and often frustrating. They need to know that they are on the right track.
- **When** is feedback most beneficial? Feedback comes in many shapes and sizes. It is up to the teacher to decide when and how much feedback will work for each child. The best time is during a teachable moment when the child has demonstrated a strategy or skill that you have been trying to teach him or her.
- **How** is feedback given? This is the most difficult part, because a delicate balance is required. If too much praise is given or if children feel that the praise is not genuine, it will be dismissed by the children. If positive feedback is given sparingly, children may not gain a true sense of how they are doing and whether you want them to do it again or not.

Creating a balance between when, where, and how feedback is given is one of the greatest challenges for all teachers. What I know for sure is that some children need a "big splash" once in a while to confirm their attempts at difficult tasks. Standing on a chair and clapping for kids *works*. If you don't believe me, try it! Delight in seeing the gleam in the eyes of kids who look up at you. In turn, they will be giving some meaningful, loving feedback back to you.

2

Catch a
Falling Reader by . . .

Using the Power of the Book Choice

> *If children could work on literature tasks most of the time, at a level of success, we would have solved the biggest problem in learning to read and write.*
>
> —Don Holdaway

Have you ever watched a big, fluffy caterpillar walk on the beach? You would be amazed at the way it travels on the sand. Its legs work in unison to pull itself up to the top of a little sand hill. Once on top, it slides down the other side of the hill and immediately heads for another hill to climb. After struggling to the top again, it slides down the other side. The caterpillar continues its journey in this same fashion. This determined little creature never once chooses to walk on a flat or smooth area of sand. It appears as if it purposely climbs up each little sand hill so that it can experience the ride down on the other side!

As I consider the journey of the caterpillar, I am reminded of how important the book choice is when working with falling readers. Choosing books that are geared to children's needs and interests is essential if we hope to move them forward in their journey to literacy. Books that *simultaneously* support and challenge the reader are ideal because they provide a way to work up the hill while also making it possible to slide down the hill.

Here are three important things to remember when choosing books for struggling readers:

1. Books that are *easy* for the reader are good for providing practice and for maintaining learned strategies. *Easy* means being able to read the majority of a book independently with accuracy and comprehension.

2. Books that are *just right* keep the reader climbing and sliding in a dance that keeps success levels high. *Just right* means that there will be opportunities for instructional assistance while providing practice with previously learned strategies and skills.

3. Books that are *too hard* should be avoided as tools for teaching children to read. *Too hard* means needing assistance with every few words while also having difficulty understanding the meaning of the text.

Remember the caterpillar's journey on the beach when selecting books for readers. Without the joy of sliding downhill, the climb up to the top would not be worth the effort. On the other hand, without the challenge of climbing uphill, there would be no joyful slide downhill. The work involved in mastering small challenges actually enables us to enjoy the feeling of success that accompanies mastery.

Choose books wisely. They are our most important tools for teaching kids to read.

3

Catch a
Falling Reader by . . .

Adjusting Our Tone of Voice . . . Frequently

Each of us has a spark of life inside us, and our highest endeavor ought to be to set off that spark in one another.

—Kenny Ausubel

What's the spark that can ignite a falling reader's brain to action? It's our voice! It is powerful, and we need to use it wisely and cleverly so that we can set off sparks in our children. What is a spark, after all? It can be described as a quick flash of light that sets something into motion or action.

By lighting sparks in the brains of our falling readers, we are constantly exciting them. The excitement that is generated raises confidence, encourages risk taking, and supports them in moving forward.

Reflect on the pitch and tone of your voice when you speak. As parents and teachers, we often express ourselves using the tone of our voices. When we're tired and stressed, kids know it. When we're happy and relaxed, they hear it in our voices. They're just like little puppies who respond to the *tone* of a voice more than what is actually said. Consider this for a moment: Would you like to listen to your voice all day long if you were a student in your classroom? Most people tell me no!

What is really meant by adjusting the tone of one's voice to prompt children during reading instruction? The keys are inflection, expression, volume, and your smile! Let's take a peek at each one of these:

- *Inflection:* The emphasis we place on certain words sends different messages. For example, you could ask the question "How do you know?" in four completely different ways depending on which word you emphasize. You could ask, "*How* do you know?" "How do *you* know?" "How *do* you know?" "How do you *know?*" Each time, the question is interpreted differently, yet it is the same question!

- *Expression:* This is so important because we can encourage, discourage, promote, or doubt children simply by the way we express ourselves verbally. We could use a different expression for the word "Oh," and it could be interpreted in a totally different way, every single time! Teachers who use a variety of expressions in their voices tend to keep kids engaged longer.

- *Volume:* Once again, kids know how we're feeling or what we're thinking just by the volume of our voices. They can tell when we're rushed, excited, sad, happy, and frustrated. If we use volume wisely, we can keep kids on their toes and use our voice to keep them focused and on task. If you're constantly shouting "Wash your hands for dinner" or "Line up for recess," using the same volume every day, guess what happens? Right—you're quickly ignored! Try whispering, speaking in a high voice, hiccupping between words, mouthing the words with no sound, or talking with a paper towel roll in front of your mouth. You'll get their attention *fast!*

- *Smile:* Huh? What's my smile got to do with my voice? Everything! Have you ever tried recording your answering machine message without smiling and then rerecording it while smiling? If not, try it! There's an amazing difference in the sound of your voice the minute you start smiling!

People actually respond better to those who are smiling while talking on the phone. For students, the combination of your voice and your smile builds support, friendship, comfort, and trust. If you're smiling and speaking in a tone that suggests "I believe in you," kids will respect and adore you. Then they will want to learn from you.

Finding out just how creative and powerful you can be simply by adjusting the tone of your voice can be incredibly exciting. Remember, it's *you* who motivates and catches kids from falling— not the books, programs, teaching tools, or creative ideas. Those things certainly can help, but *you* are the one to whom the child is responding. Your voice is a very important part of you, and it can serve as a hook for catching falling readers. *Use it!*

4

Catch a
Falling Reader by . . .

Making Eye Contact at Teachable Moments

Better than a thousand days of diligent study is one day with a great teacher.

—Japanese proverb

W e have fewer than 180 days to work some miracles for some kids. We have no time to lose, and we can't afford to let them wander away during critical teaching moments. What do I mean by "wander away"? I'm referring to behaviors that take the focus away from the lesson, activity, or teaching point we're trying to make. Here are a few common wandering behaviors that you may be all too familiar with:

- Looking up at the lights or out the window
- Focusing on a tiny speck of paper or object on the floor
- Flipping a pencil or eraser in the air
- Doodling on the desk or on the outside of a book
- Tapping or drumming

- Wriggling, coughing, blinking, or stretching
- Playing with shoelaces, buttons, hair, jewelry, and so on

Let's face it: children who wander away tend to have short attention spans, and this makes it extra challenging for teachers. These wanderers have little patience, and they often grow bored and apathetic about learning. They become easily frustrated because they may not get it right away, and so they start to find ways to entertain themselves.

In the meantime, the teacher proceeds with the lesson, hoping that falling kids will get something out of it. Unfortunately, all these kids are doing is tuning out and wandering further and further away until they are so far behind that they can't possibly catch up.

Eye contact is powerful and effective. If you are not using it to your advantage, reflect on this as you work with struggling kids. Through our eyes, we convey messages that can catch kids before, during, or after they wander. We can smile with our eyes, search with our eyes, believe with our eyes, and share with our eyes.

When we look directly into the eyes of children, we send the message, "I need your attention and you have mine!" We focus the children on what we want them to hear, and we convey a feeling of caring. Kids respond to caring, and they are especially attuned to the feedback given to them through the eyes of their caretakers.

Feedback comes in different packages, and exceptional teachers find a variety of ways to offer it. Too often, we talk to the top of kids' heads. We might stop and stand near a child who is reading, offer a brief word of praise, but then stop in the middle of our sentence to look toward the back of the room and shout, "What's happening back there at the computer? Mark, why are you walking around with nothing to do? Where's your pencil?" Then we move on to the next child without realizing that the feedback we just offered was totally ineffective for the child who was sitting under us while we were shouting across the room. We've all done it at one time or another.

Now, what would happen if we had stooped to the eye level of the child who was reading, smiled into their eyes, and said, "Yes! You went back to the beginning of the line. That's what good readers do! Keep going . . . you're doing great!" Now that's feedback! How engaged do you think kids would be in a small group lesson if you were standing and moving your head down to them just as they began to wander? How fast could you pull kids back into a lesson if you were on the floor across from them so that you could catch their eyes at a teachable moment?

Get to the eyes, you get to the brain! If you don't believe me, just try it. You'll be amazed at the level of engagement that you can commend simply by using your eyes. You don't want to do it every minute, nor do you want to come on too strong with shy or reserved kids. You also want to be cautious about eye contact with autistic or special needs students unless it is recommended by trained professionals. Finally, you don't want to use eye contact in place of "teaching from behind." But there are moments when eye contact can make a huge difference in making a point and in offering the kind of feedback that shows you care while also demanding that the child care too.

Want to ignite the spark in your learner's eyes? Use your eyes to keep kids from wandering away from you. After a little practice with eye contact, you will see the light go on in the eyes of a child who lost it. What great feedback that is . . . for you!

5

Catch a
Falling Reader by . . .

Adjusting the Pace of Each Lesson

Start out fast and keep trying to pick up speed. Then leave skid marks!

—Rudy Crew, former chancellor for
New York City Schools

Have you ever listened to Beethoven's Fifth Symphony? If you have, you will probably agree that it is one of the greatest symphonies of all time. I believe that one of the strengths of this great work is the pace that Beethoven created throughout each movement. One minute it is fast and loud, then quiet and thoughtful. You find your heartbeat racing during the parts where the rhythm of the drums are engaging you to interact. You find yourself humming the beautiful melody of the third movement because of its gentle flowing quality. The pace of this incredible symphony keeps you on the edge of your seat. It hooks you in the beginning, keeps you motivated throughout the middle parts, and brings you to the top of the highest mountain when it ends.

What can we learn from Beethoven, besides the essence of musical excellence? *Pace makes a difference!* I would argue that even with the exact same notes and instruments, Beethoven's Fifth Symphony would not have been the same without careful attention to pace. Now we start, now we stop. Now we start, now we stop.

The ability to use pace to one's advantage is part of the craft of teaching—the art, if you will. Pace and timing are not things that can be taught in an education course. They certainly can be modeled and promoted, but taught? I think not.

I call your attention to this important aspect of teaching because it makes a difference when catching falling kids. Many of these children are so easily distracted and their minds are filled with noise. They find it hard to concentrate for a host of reasons. We can't change those reasons, but we can adjust our pace until we perfect the craft of engaging kids.

Consider the following options for using pace to your advantage:

- *Wait Time:* Are you giving kids time to think and problem solve before you jump in to help them?
- *Feedback:* Are you offering positive feedback just at the moment when the readers do something you have taught them to do? A simple "yes" in their ear is sufficient and very effective. You can do this without breaking the flow of the sentence or story, if you practice. You don't, however, want to overdo it, as it will lose its effectiveness.
- *Voice:* Does your voice command that kids engage with you, or is it too slow and soft? You can adjust your pace by using your voice in creative ways. If you're not sure how to do that, watch public television shows for young children. Puppets' voices are used in a variety of engaging ways, keeping the pace moving throughout each segment. How else would one keep a toddler glued to a television for an hour?
- *Body Language:* Are you standing up, crouching down, moving to the back of the room, waving your arms, using your hands, and adjusting your facial expressions to change the pace? Sitting at a table or in a chair the majority

of times can suggest passivity, and many kids will seize upon this to misbehave.

- *Speed:* Are you moving the lesson along so that kids don't have time to blink, yawn, and fall on the floor, or go to the bathroom?! I am not advocating that we race through every lesson. Rather, I am suggesting that we pick up the pace a bit, especially for kids who are frustrated. Kids will often tell us that they are "always waiting for something to happen or for someone to get ready." This waiting around often disengages learners from the learning process and for some kids can be an invitation to misbehave.

Today's kids can and do respond well to a pace that creates a sense of urgency and mental stimulation. If you don't believe me, just watch children while they are playing a fast-paced board game, a video game, pinball machine, or a computer-generated activity. They stay engaged and focused if the pace is just right—not too slow and not too fast. Choosing to adjust your pace in a variety of creative ways can help you move falling readers along at a good pace!

6

Catch a
Falling Reader by . . .

Using Different Forms of Feedback

An unhatched egg is to me the greatest challenge in life.

—E. B. White

If you look up the word "feedback" in a thesaurus, you will find several other words that can be used in place of that one: "criticism," "advice," "pointer," "reaction," "comment," "response," "opinion," "view." Now, let's reflect on these a minute, because as teachers and parents, we are constantly offering feedback to kids— good, bad, or indifferent. Amazingly, kids are extremely in tune with the underlying messages that lie beneath the actual feedback that is given. Here's where we need to be careful when it comes to falling kids. We simply cannot afford to add to their frustration or to complicate their learning process by sending negative feedback.

This is not to say that we purposely send negative feedback to struggling kids. It's merely a reminder that sometimes, either because we don't have time to think about *how* we're sharing feedback or because our words said one thing but our voice and body language said another, kids sometimes get the wrong feedback. This can move falling kids backward, whereas we want to keep them moving forward.

Here are five questions to ask yourself as you reflect on the way you give feedback to kids:

1. What's the reaction of my falling kids when I offer them feedback?

2. What message is my body conveying when I respond, react, and engage with kids?

3. What does the tone in my voice sound like when I offer praise, constructive criticism, or my opinion?

4. Am I offering feedback in a variety of ways so that it is effective in sending the message that I want to send?

5. Are kids constantly asking me for feedback? If so, why?

We all need and want feedback. It is important to our growth and development as human beings. Falling kids, however, need a careful dose of it so that they can overcome feelings of inadequacy, frustration, and low self-esteem. They do not, however, need *false feedback*. By this I mean that we should not tell kids they are right when they are not. Here's a true story to illustrate this important point:

I was observing in a second-grade classroom during writer's workshop. Kids were all writing in their journals, responding to a poem that the class had shared when the lesson began. The teacher was roaming behind children, offering support and guidance. Louis raised his hand and said, "How do you spell 'cookie'?" The teacher told him to sound it out and to write what he hears. Louis did so and then he got up and brought his journal to his teacher. He pointed to the word and said, "Is this how you spell 'cookie'?" The teacher said, "Good job!" and Louis went back to his seat. A minute later, Louis noticed me sitting in the back of the room. He got up and walked over to me, journal in hand. He whispered, "Is this really how you spell 'cookie'?" I looked at his attempt at the word. He had written "coce," and I asked, "Does it look right to you, Louis?" He said, "No." I then said, "You did a good job hearing the sounds in that word, Louis, but let me show you how it really looks." I then wrote the correct spelling for Louis on a separate piece of paper. He smiled and said "Thanks." Later that day, I popped my head back into the class to see what was happening. Louis got up from the group circle, put his arms around my waist, and whispered, "Thank you for helping me with that word."

True story. Validate the attempts that kids make, but give them feedback that will help them become independent, risk-taking, confident learners!

7

Catch a Falling Reader by . . .

Setting a Purpose for Reading

Few things can help an individual more than to place respon-sibility on him, and to let him know that you trust him.

—Booker T. Washington,
reformer, educator, and author

Ever wonder why traditional reading program manuals have always instructed teachers to have kids read to a page number? When you really think about it, we never read up to a specific page number. The whole purpose of reading is to gain meaning from printed text. The practice of reading until you get to a certain page is one that chops up the meaning. I presume that it was instituted for the purpose of keeping all kids on the same page at the same time.

Let's consider what reading to a page number actually suggests. Some children see this as a means of getting out of reading the story in their group lesson. In other words, they often resort to "fake reading" by moving their eyes across the pages, turning the pages, and landing on the page they were instructed to read to. Honestly, if a college professor asked us to read to a certain page in a statistics text, we might actually do the same thing!

There is simply no incentive for reading to a page number, because the purposes for reading the text become unclear. Those children who lack intrinsic motivation for reading will do whatever they can to get out of the task, especially if it is difficult and frustrating. This, therefore, is the dilemma for many falling readers.

So what should we do to keep the group focused and engaged in the text? During guided small-group reading instruction, it is much more effective to ask children to read for a purpose. This gives them a mission and helps them to break the story into meaningful chunks so that comprehension can be reinforced.

Here are a few prompts that will encourage purposeful reading:

- "Read until you get to the part where _____."
- "Read to find out what happened when _____."
- "Read until you figure out the problem in the story."
- "Read up to the part where you find the solution to the problem."
- "Stop reading when you find out _____."
- "Put your finger in the page and close the book when you discover _____."
- "Flip your book over when you reach the paragraph that describes _____."
- "Read to find out where this story takes place."
- "See if you can find out what genre this text is written as. Stop when you know for sure."
- "Read until you discover whether this is a true story or not."

Once readers get to the parts that you wanted them to read to, they can do any number of things to build comprehension and oral reading fluency. Here are a few suggestions:

- Say, "Who can read the part that tells us where this story takes place?"
- Ask students to write down the problem they discovered in the story.
- Have young readers draw a "quick picture" of what they think will happen next.

- Use a chart to create a web for recording elements of the story that made it fiction or nonfiction. Ask readers to find evidence in the text to support their ideas.
- Ask a variety of questions to encourage comprehension and lead to critical thinking.
- Ask students to "read the part where _____" to a buddy next to them.
- Students can write about what they discovered, up to that point in the story, as a seat work task.

The practice of reading for a purpose is a powerful one. It motivates children who might otherwise overlook the value of reading the text. It also provides a gentle push for readers who read too quickly over material and who might otherwise skip over key messages in the story. Reading for a purpose can keep kids engaged and focused throughout the guided reading lesson. Now, wouldn't that be great!

8

Catch a Falling Reader by . . .

Stimulating and Motivating Children With Puppets

> *The happiness of life is made up of minute fractions—the little, soon-forgotten charities of a kiss or smile, a kind look or heartfelt compliment.*
>
> —Samuel Taylor Coleridge

There is more magic in a puppet than any adult could ever possibly imagine. A puppet can be a parent or teacher's best tool for motivating, teaching, and catching kids. I think the power of the puppet comes from the innate ability that children have for imagination, fun, silliness, and simplicity. Puppets do and say things that adults don't. That's the bottom line when it comes to kids. That may be why children sit still for so long when a puppet is in action.

In the case of falling readers, a puppet is most effective during those teachable moments when we want children to attend and remember. Believe it or not, kids will remember what a puppet taught them better and longer than what they learned from adults! The trick is to find a puppet that *you* feel comfortable using so that you can create a personality that will succeed in reaching your struggling learners. Actually, I do not advocate using puppets for only those who have difficulty. They are powerful and effective for *all* primary grade children.

Many people feel shy or self-conscious about using a puppet to teach with. For the sake of the kids you are trying to catch, you must set aside any reluctance and practice using the puppet to its maximum advantage. What do I mean by this? If you are uncomfortable with adapting a voice for the puppet, then just make the puppet be one that is too shy to talk. This puppet only whispers in your ear, and you respond to it as though it really did talk to you. The kids don't realize that the puppet is not actually talking. They are reacting to *your* reaction, and this makes the puppet come alive. For example, my mouse puppet, Max, was purchased with some wordless books about a silly mouse in mind. I used Max to introduce the cover, get kids to talk through the pictures, and help them make predications. Max would whisper something in my ear, and I'd turn my face, look at him, and say something like, "What's that, Max? You think this book is all about cheese? Oh, really, you character! Show me how in the world you got that idea from the cover of the book! Oh, Max, you are so obsessed with cheese. What? You found cheese in our principal's sock drawer? What in the world were you doing in there?!" At this point, the kids are absolutely hysterical with laughter. They then proceed to explain to Max what this book is really about, based on the title and cover pictures.

It's very hard to write about how to use a puppet. It comes from inside of you, and this is where all your power is! At strategic moments, you can catch a child's attention by pulling out a puppet and making a key point. You can reinforce these teaching points with the puppet whenever the teachable moment arises. You can also use the puppet as a way for kids to describe how they feel, what they've learned, or what good readers do when they come to difficult words. In other words, kids will very patiently talk to a puppet, and this reinforces what they know. This also gives them a chance to express themselves orally in a nonthreatening, comfortable manner.

Next time you're stuck on that rocking chair with a child whom you can't seem to move forward, pull out a puppet and watch the child come to life. Remember that the puppet can reach the child only through you. You know the child, so use the puppet to touch the child in ways that only puppets can!

9

Catch a
Falling Reader by . . .

Using Physical Actions to Help Kids Remember

It is the supreme art of the teacher to awaken joy in creative expression and knowledge.

—Albert Einstein

We all have different ways of remembering different things. Do you remember how you memorized the names of the Great Lakes or the planets? Some of our teachers gave us mnemonic ways of remembering the things that were difficult to recall at a moment's notice. In many cases, we can still remember these facts or bits of knowledge solely because we committed them to our long-term memory by attaching them to something that we *could* remember.

Many falling kids struggle with their memories. There are any numbers of neurological, developmental, environmental, and genetic reasons why certain kids just can't remember or recall certain things. They find it difficult to make connections on their own, and this leads to frustration, disappointment, and defeat. It is our task to make the connections for these kids so that they can begin to use them in moving forward with their literacy skills.

One important way to help children is to attach a physical action to whatever we want them to recall or remember. Here are a few examples of actions that you might use to help falling readers remember the things you are teaching them:

Vowel Sounds:

- Short *a*: "Hold a pretend flashlight up to your mouth and say 'aaaah,' just like you would if a doctor looked in your throat. Every time you need to know that short *a* sound, hold the flashlight up to your mouth and say 'aaaah.'"
- Short *e*: "Say 'elephant.' Now let's say it again and hold that short *e* sound for a long time. Take your pointer finger and make a pretend line with your finger in front of your mouth to show me the shape of your mouth when you say *e* like in 'elephant.' Your finger is moving in a straight line, left to right. That's the same way we start out writing the letter *e*. So, if you get stuck on that sound, see if your mouth is making a straight line and then write the letter *e*. They should match!"
- Short *i*: "With your two pointer fingers, push your cheeks up as you say 'igloo.' Your cheeks want to go up on that first *i* part, don't they? Let's try another one. Push your cheeks up toward your eyes when you say 'it,' 'in,' 'if.' Remember to check your cheeks when you're trying to figure out the short *i* sound."
- Short *o*: "What is your mouth doing when you say the short *o* sound in 'hot,' 'pot,' 'box'? Trace your mouth when you say that sound. What letter are you making? Yes! An *o*! Check your mouth each time you wonder which vowel sound you need."
- Short *u*: "Take your fist and gently punch your tummy. What sound would you probably make if you really punched it? *Uhhhh!* Yes! Now, let's try 'bus.' As you say that middle sound, bring your fist toward your stomach while you say the 'uhhh' sound. That will help you remember the short *u* sound if you hear it in a word. Don't really punch yourself!"

It is truly amazing to look around the room and see kids actually using these physical actions to remember short vowel sounds in words they are trying to read and write. If you have modeled, practiced, and insisted that they apply these to new and difficult words, they will begin to independently apply these physical actions as a way of remembering "hard things." If you don't believe me, try them and see what happens! Falling kids need whole hosts of ways to remember what many of us take for granted.

10

Catch a
Falling Reader by . . .

Creating Bridges for Kids

He that would be a leader must be a bridge.

—Welsh proverb

What does a bridge actually do? It connects two places that may otherwise be hard to get to. A bridge is created to help us get from one place to the other. For kids who begin to fall, we must start to build bridges quickly. If they can't move from one place to another, they lose motivation. This often creates a downward spiral that is hard to reverse. Falling kids need bridges, and it's up to us to create them daily. Let's look at why this is important.

So many children simply cannot make connections between what they are learning and why they need to know what they're learning. If something has no value to me or if I can't see the value in learning it, I won't invest time and energy into truly learning it. If there's no value in learning this, then why should I attend to it? Why should I invest my time and effort into learning it? Consequently, performing a task or participating in a lesson is done because someone else told me to do it and that someone else is in a position of authority, so I'd better do it!

Here's a true story to illustrate this point. Young learners are working with a teacher in a small group. The teacher has a large chart on the floor. On the chart are three categories: Air, Water, and Land. There are lines to separate these categories. The teacher asks children to help her put the right figurines into the right categories. She holds up a plastic horse and the children say, "Put it under Land." She holds up a small airplane and says, "Where should we put this one?" The kids shout, "Air." Now in theory, this is a wonderful lesson for teaching children to search for common characteristics and then categorize items. The problem, however, is that these children had no idea why they were doing this, nor was there any connection to why they needed to know this. They simply participated in this planned activity and then got up and went to other activities around the room. When I asked some of the children in this group why their teacher had them do that activity, many simply answered, "I don't know. We just did it." What good is the wonderful activity if a bridge is not created to the actual learning outcome for the activity?

If we don't make connections for children and give them real reasons for why they need to learn what we're trying to teach them, they will simply do it because they were told to. This leaves them with fragmented pieces and isolated skills. As teachers and parents, we must strive to connect what we want kids to know with *why* we want them to know it.

In the lesson described above, it would have been much more meaningful if a bridge had been created for these children. The lesson could have begun with a lively discussion of how grocery stores are organized. Most kids know grocery stores. They can come to understand why categorizing items and foods is necessary and important. They can then be led to analyze characteristics of foods in order to put them into a category. This understanding is supported by the Land, Air, and Water activity. Once the activity is over, we must create a bridge for students so that they see the value of knowing how to categorize items. For instance, we might ask them to check out their kitchen cupboards and make a list of how things are sorted in these cupboards. The same idea could be applied to our dresser drawers or the books in the school library.

Creating bridges is a vital part of what we, as teachers and parents, do if we are to move kids forward. So many falling kids cannot make connections on their own, for a million complex reasons. When we create bridges for kids, we give them reasons to attend, to engage, and to apply what we're teaching them. Think back to the best teachers in your life. I guarantee that they created bridges for you so you could cross from one place to another.

Leaders of kids must create bridges for kids!

Part II

Instructional Strategies Produce Results

As educators, we are given 180 or fewer school days per year to work a miracle with so many of our falling kids! Therefore, we must strive to learn and apply the most effective instructional strategies possible, constantly adding to our teaching toolbox. This section supplies the reader with a variety of instructional strategies, approaches, and ideas for giving falling readers what they need to progress on their path to literacy. Teachers and reading specialists are advised to try these suggestions *many* times in *many* ways with *many* students. We all learn how to do things best when we have opportunities to practice what we learn and then to share what we have learned with others.

Catch a Falling Reader by . . . *Teaching From "Behind" the Child*
Catch a Falling Reader by . . . *Utilizing Wordless Books to Increase Language Skills*
Catch a Falling Reader by . . . *Modeling What Good Readers Do*
Catch a Falling Reader by . . . *Using a Clipboard for Tricky Words*
Catch a Falling Reader by . . . *Teaching Them How to Think as They Read*

Catch a Falling Reader by . . . *Using Magnetic Letters in a Variety of Ways*

Catch a Falling Reader by . . . *Writing Words FAST*

Catch a Falling Reader by . . . *Engaging Learners With an Overhead Projector*

Catch a Falling Reader by . . . *Encouraging Repeated Readings*

Catch a Falling Reader by . . . *Establishing and Supporting a Daily Block of Reading Time*

Catch a Falling Reader by . . . *Teaching Kids How to Use a Listening Center*

Catch a Falling Reader by . . . *Building Fluency in a Variety of Ways*

Catch a Falling Reader by . . . *Using Focus Sheets and Graphic Organizers to Link Writing to Reading*

Catch a Falling Reader by . . . *Providing Engaging Learning Center Activities*

Catch a Falling Reader by . . . *Interacting With Kids as They Write*

Catch a Falling Reader by . . . *Providing Daily Read-Alouds*

11

Catch a
Falling Reader by . . .

Teaching From "Behind" the Child

I cannot judge my work while I am doing it. I have to do as painters do, stand back and view it from a distance, but not too great a distance.

—Blaise Pascal

The idea of teaching from "behind" the child during reading instruction is a fairly new one. We have traditionally taught from the front of the room, above a group of children, and across from them. When we stand behind children as they read and write, we send several important messages to the child (especially to falling readers):

1. I am here to guide you and to act as your coach.

2. *You* are in control of the text and the challenges before you.

3. I am not checking up on you. I am merely observing how you are doing.

4. You are capable of reading this book all by yourself! I believe in you.

As teachers and parents observe children from a distance, there is time to really think about what the child can do and what the child needs. This drives our next steps and helps us to know which verbal prompts to use when coaching the child. This is important because so many of us instinctively want to jump in the minute a child begins to struggle. Sometimes we are too quick to tell children the first sound and even the word they're stuck on. Every time this happens, children become more and more dependent on others for assistance.

Consider the following suggestions while standing behind the reader (not necessarily in this order):

- Provide some "wait time." Give readers some time to *think* for a few seconds before prompting them.
- Tell children to make the first sound and to try it.
- Ask children to find a part of the word they know.
- Break the word up for children with your thumb and then move their thumb to do the same.
- Point to the picture and then back to the beginning sound. Tell children "Now you try it."
- Remind children to go back to the beginning of the line and start again.
- Offer children three choices: "Could it be ____?" "Could it be ____?" "Could it be ____?"
- Ask "How can you help yourself?"
- If the prompts are not working, simply tell children the word so they can move on without breaking the flow of the sentence.

Think of teaching from behind as a powerful way to become the reader's Jiminy Cricket. Remember how Jiminy sat on Pinocchio's shoulder and whispered into his ear? He offered advice, support, encouragement, praise, and direction.

This is exactly what falling readers need on a daily basis. Their brains are *not* automatically telling them what strategies and skills to apply when things get difficult. Acting as a Jiminy Cricket for the child can kick the brain into action. With enough coaching and support, children begin to internalize the prompts that you have been teaching them. In other words, the falling reader starts to fly upward. Now self-esteem is elevated, confidence is restored, and the train can move forward!

***Become a wise and clever Jiminy
Cricket and see what happens!***

12

Catch a
Falling Reader by . . .

Utilizing Wordless Books to Increase Language Skills

> *When we try to provide experiences that will compensate for limited language learning opportunities, we must go beyond the usual bounds of spontaneous learning in a free play group situation. . . . We should arrange for language-producing activities.*
>
> —Marie M. Clay

Every falling reader is filled with a variety of experiences, skills, behaviors, backgrounds, feelings, and roots. One of the things I want to know about any struggling reader is his or her language base. What is meant by the term "language base"? It refers to a child's ability to communicate using spoken words. This includes description, prediction, vocabulary usage, grammatical structures, word retrieval, and conversation. Falling readers are often falling because of a limited language base when they enter school.

Language activities must extend beyond casual conversations, short retellings, and literal questions. They must supply an *interactive exchange* of thoughts and ideas between the adult and child. Wordless picture books can promote this exchange effectively. Adults and children can collectively share their ideas, opinions, past experiences, predictions, knowledge of vocabulary and sentence structure, descriptive language, and much more.

Let's explore some of the benefits to using wordless books for instruction:

- When young children are asked to describe the plot of a story or to make predictions, based on pictures alone, they are asked to call upon their own personal storehouse of vocabulary and past experiences. This can be valuable information in planning for instruction.
- Second-language learners can benefit from language activities that enrich their vocabulary, expand their understandings of concepts, and support grammatical sentence structures.
- Teachers and parents will gain valuable insights about what children can do through observation of how children use language, draw from prior knowledge, pronounce sounds in words, and apply book handling skills.
- Shy or introverted children tend to forget themselves when "telling the story" with a wordless book. They are free to express themselves without judgment, criticism, or "right answers."
- Children with limited book experiences can benefit from reading the pictures without feeling pressured actually to *read* the words.
- Early concepts about print can be reinforced quickly and easily. These concepts include book handling skills, directionality, use of the title and cover, attention to details, picture clues, and matching the word to the picture by pointing and saying.
- Young readers can learn to predict the sequence of events in a wordless book and to really *think* about what's happening in the story.

- Children who dislike writing stories or have trouble "thinking of something to write about" can use stories in wordless books to stimulate ideas while also serving as a framework for sequential events and text structure.
- Increased development of word retrieval skills, sentence structure, and vocabulary can promote successful reading fluency.
- By using wordless books as springboards for shared reading and writing experiences, children can truly see the powerful reciprocity between reading and writing.

Here are a few suggestions for reading wordless picture books together:

- Discuss the title and cover picture. Ask, "What is this story about? What do you notice about the picture?"
- Begin reading the story to the child by modeling a complete sentence. For example, "One day, a bird was sitting in a tree and it saw a big red apple fall."
- Let the child tell the story. Encourage him or her to speak in complete sentences. Take turns doing this if it is difficult for the child. Encourage descriptive talk: "What color is it? Where is it? What else can we say about this dog? Is it big, small, happy, and sad?"
- Ask your young reader to make predictions in between pages by asking, "What do you think might happen next?" "Can you guess what they might do on the next page?" "Do you think they are happy?" "How do you know?" "Does this remind you of anything?"
- Encourage the child to reread the whole story to you, without questions or interruptions.
- After the reading, the child may want to dictate a sentence or story to you about the book. You (or the child) can write the story on paper and the child can draw or paint a picture to go with it.

Falling readers, as well as all young learners, can benefit from using wordless books in a variety of creative ways. Remember, a picture is worth a thousand words.

13

Catch a
Falling Reader by . . .

Modeling What Good Readers Do

Give a man a fish, you feed him for a day. Teach him how to fish, you feed him for a lifetime.

—Lao Tzu

We all learn by observing what competent, successful people do. For instance, we learn skills and strategies by watching good cooks, we adapt new moves from observing good skiers, and we can learn from the experiences and hardships of good dieters. Children need to know what good readers and writers do. If they have grown up without daily modeling of language and literacy skills, they will need to know these things even more than others if they hope to catch up to their peers.

When we engage children in the practice of shared reading, we involve them in the very things that good readers do. We model good reading while also drawing them into the act of reading. Big books and enlarged texts are perfect for this because they are usually read with the whole group. This gives struggling kids a chance to learn from their teacher as well as their peers. It also provides a nonthreatening context for practicing quietly by participating in the best way you know how. The key to success is in knowing how to model what good readers do without putting kids on the spot in front of their peers.

Here are a few tips for sharing language and literacy experiences together while also modeling the ways of good readers:

- Get in the habit of saying, "Good for you! That's what good readers do!" or "I like the way you all used your eyes to point to the words, just like good readers do!" These powerful statements will stick in the heads of kids because they know what your expectations are. Verbal prompts might include something like, "You went back when you got stuck. That's what good readers do," and "Yes, you left spaces between your words! That's what good writers do." These statements not only confirm the reader's action or behavior, but they also encourage the child to keep moving forward. Once again, this is feedback. If used frequently and wisely, it can catch kids and pull them up . . . fast! It is psychologically similar to what might happen if someone said to us, "Good for you. You're doing what good dieters do in order to keep that weight off." We would more than likely feel that our efforts were noticed and then confirmed. We all need to know if we are on the right track. So do kids!

- Set up a "working" listening center in your classroom or home. This means that the headphones and CD players are in good working order! Then be sure to have a variety of books and CDs for kids to listen to. When readers record books on audio, they read faster and more fluently than young readers read. This is good modeling. It also forces the child to visually scan across the lines and subsequent lines more quickly. With practice, scanning abilities become second nature, and most readers no longer need to use their fingers or a bookmark to track the lines. Falling readers should be listening to books and CDs *daily*. They should also be given opportunities to respond to the book they listened to through creative art and writing activities. Respond sheets, graphic organizers, and story frames all lend themselves well to extending readers beyond just *listening* to a book and CD, although just listening has its place too.

Children who are not read to or told stories will greatly benefit from the rich language experiences that can be gained from listening to audiobooks.

- Buddy reading is an effective way for readers to learn from each other. Pairing up children in various ways can lead to modeling and sharing that might otherwise be lost in the shuffle of everyday classroom life. Just as babies love to watch and learn from toddlers, readers can learn much from sharing literacy experiences with their peers. This is *not* to say, however, that advanced readers should *always* be paired with falling readers. This is a good practice when children are encouraged to build on each other's strengths. If it becomes common practice, then struggling kids often resent the fact that they can't read like their buddy. Common sense should guide you in pairing students up in a variety of ways. Struggling kids can coach and help each other as well! They should also have opportunities to be shining stars, and this may mean that they should have buddies who are younger than them once in a while. There is great power in having a falling reader read to a preschooler or kindergarten buddy. The little ones will also be getting the modeling they need as well.

Perhaps one of the greatest teaching tools available to anyone who teaches is the ability to model. Master this, and you will catch many kids who might otherwise continue to founder, all the while looking for someone to actually show them how it's done.

14

Catch a
Falling Reader by . . .

Using a Clipboard for Tricky Words

Even today, when I can't figure out a word, I guess from the context. Yes, I guess what makes sense.

—Baruj Benacerraf, immunologist

Have you ever wondered why publishers list all the words that should be introduced to children before they read? I have. If we tell children all the words that may be difficult when they first attempt a story, we are robbing them of the opportunity to problem solve on their own. We may actually be keeping them from using the very strategies and skills that we are teaching them to use.

That's not to say that we shouldn't introduce and discuss vocabulary that is crucial to the content of the story or foreign to most kids. We would be wise to use our discretion regarding words that we need to introduce before readers read. Having said this, I recommend that we encourage falling readers to take a more active role in identifying words that were tricky *to them.* Then we should guide them to identify which strategy they used to solve that tricky word.

The practice of using a clipboard to identify tricky words and strategies is a good one for some kids. Just as with all practices, this one should not be used for *all* kids, nor should it be employed every day. Techniques lose their appeal and power when they are overused. This particular practice is most effective with readers who tend to ignore strategies that have been taught. It helps them tune into words that need extra attention and then identify the strategy or behavior that was used to solve that word.

Here's how it's done:

1. Each student in the reading group is given a clipboard and a form to write on. The form has horizontal lines on it with an inch of space between the lines. This gives the child space to write.

2. The story is introduced and students participate in guided reading, with the teacher coaching in a variety of ways. Young readers should be encouraged to "read to their ear" so they don't disturb others around them but they can still be heard by the teacher.

3. After the reading of the text, the readers discuss the story and the tricky words. The teacher tells each child to identify one or two words that were new or difficult and asks them to think about how that word was solved. In the space provided on the form, the child then writes the word on the clipboard along with the strategy used to figure out that word. For example, the reader might say that the word "standing" was tricky. He figured out that word by chunking it—looking for known parts ("and," "stand," "ing") and then putting it all together. So the child would list the strategy of chunking the word on the clipboard.

4. It is important that the student understand the meaning of the word as well. We should guide children in discussing the meaning of tricky words and perhaps using the word in a new sentence in order to cement the meaning. What good is the ability to decode words if the meaning is lost?

The act of writing things down tends to bring them to a conscious level. Isn't that what dieters do when they're on weight loss programs? Write the strategies down. Write them down! Write them down! Why? The act of writing something down can often lead to conscious awareness, and this awareness can bring about a lasting change in behavior.

Once again, we must be careful not to do this too often, because we don't want kids stopping to tell us how they got words. We ultimately want them to read fluently and not worry about how they got the words. However, the practice of using a clipboard to write the word and the strategy used might just work for falling readers who are ignoring strategies when solving print problems.

Try it and see what happens.

15

Catch a
Falling Reader by . . .

Teaching Them How to Think as They Read

Teach students how to ask questions in a manner that leads to the answer, and you will be teaching them the answer.

—Anonymous

One of the greatest things we can do for kids is to teach them how to ask questions of themselves as they are reading. The trick is to use the power of modeling, and no program or set of materials can do this for you. It is the teacher who models strategies, behaviors, and skills. It is the teacher who demonstrates how to do something, not the program that is sitting on the shelf. Just as effective ski instructors use the power of demonstration to teach their students, teachers and parents must also do the same.

What does this sort of modeling look like? It starts with a willingness to verbalize and share our own thinking with the kids. For example, we might start them out by saying, "Today, we're going to think through this book together, and I will be telling you what I'm thinking about as well." This introduction sets up the thinking and establishes a purpose for the lesson. As the adult reads the text aloud, he or she stops at certain places to think out loud. Here are a few key phrases that might be used to model the process of thinking and questioning a text as it is read:

- "I'm wondering . . ."
- "This part has me confused. Let's look at the words in the story that might clear up this confusion."
- "So now I understand that . . ."
- "Listen to the words that helped me." (Teacher points to the actual page and then reads the supporting evidence aloud.)
- "I don't understand why . . . Can someone help me think through this part of the story?"
- "Here's a question that keeps coming back at me as I read."
- "This is a sentence that still has me baffled. What do you think it really means?"
- "How can this be true? I'm wondering if I should believe everything that I read."
- "When did that take place? Here are the words that answer that question."
- "What is this author really trying to say? Let me read on before I figure that one out."
- "I still don't get this part. Let me go back and see what happened earlier in the story."
- "This is puzzling to me. What can I do to figure it out?"
- "Wait a minute! Now I see what's going on. Listen to this part."

It is important that the tone of the voice be considered whenever we are modeling our questions aloud for kids. Little puppies and kids are especially gifted in picking up on what we mean simply by the tone in our voice. We can sound genuinely curious or ridiculously bored depending on how we ask the question. Teaching kids to think while reading is a monumental task because it requires that we share our personal thoughts, ideas, confusions, and strategies.

The ultimate goal is to problem solve comprehension skills aloud so that kids will begin to take risks, ask questions inside their heads and in their writing, and justify their answers with evidence from the text. A whole-group 15-minute lesson works well for this type of activity. Watch the results blossom as your kids begin to think when they read and write. Kids, after all, are naturally curious. Let's hope that we are building on that natural ability so that we can encourage the act of thinking.

Wouldn't it be refreshing if people actually got paid just to think?

16

Catch a
Falling Reader by . . .

Using Magnetic Letters in a Variety of Ways

Everything you do changes your brain and the changes in your brain change you!

—Eric Jensen

What is the magic behind our little colored magnetic letters? How can we use them to teach kids how words work? What is the role of the teacher when using magnetic letters with falling readers? Good questions! Magnetic letters provide opportunities for a tactile, kinesthetic approach to learning about letters and sounds within words. The very act of making and breaking words with real letters is powerful and should be used daily with struggling kids.

I think the magic of these little letters lies in the numerous possibilities for teaching kids to be flexible and successful at the same time. Flexibility occurs when we expect the child to use these letters in a variety of ways to create and build new words. Success is achieved by starting from what the child knows and working from there to create new understanding. The combination of flexibility and success can lead to proficiency, if done consistently.

We utilize magnetic letters to teach phonetic skills by focusing on commonalities among words. This is only possible once kids know the names and sounds of the letters. Toddlers and preschoolers can benefit from using magnetic letters on their refrigerator door or on magnetic white boards while sitting in the car. They should be sorting and categorizing letters so that they become familiar and able to start building words with them. Sorting letters can be done using hula hoops, muffin tins, or cookie sheets. You will want to use lowercase magnetic letters since these are the letters that are most often used!

Kids can sort letters using the following categories:

- Uppercase and lowercase letters
- Letters that have half circles
- Letters versus numbers
- Letters that have sticks
- Letters that have a circle and a stick
- Vowels versus consonants
- Red letters and blue letters

There are plenty of good books on the market that offer ideas for teaching young learners about letters and sounds. The next step is to move children to make and break words. We always start with what children know, and this is most easily discovered by looking at words they can write. For instance, if you know that children can write the word "and," you can begin by having them build that word with letters. Then add a magnetic *s* to the board and ask them to say and make "sand." If they put the *s* in the wrong place, scramble the letters and ask them to go and make "and." You always want to return to what is known and build from there. That is a critical point.

As children begin to build words in a variety of flexible ways, we want to link these skills with real reading and writing. You should call attention to known parts or chunks within words *as* kids are reading. For example, when coming to the word "standing," say, "What do you notice about that word? Show me the little chunk you know in that word by taking your two pointer fingers and framing it like this." The teacher will frame the chunk "and." Then ask children to do the same. Now say, "Do you see another chunk in that word that you know?" Move them to finding "ing." This will then lead them to applying the beginning sounds to the known chunks. If not, have them make "and" on their desks with magnetic letters. Then offer them an *s* to make "sand," next a *t* to make "stand," and finally the "ing" chunk. Go back to the text and have them reread the sentence, applying the strategies you have just taught.

The role of the teacher is critical in the process of teaching kids how words work. The teacher's voice, pace, and knowledge of what the child knows are all essential. We must create a fun but effective way to teach falling readers about the code. If the activity is too slow or too easy, these kids will instantly turn off to the whole thing. If it's too difficult, they will lose motivation. The challenge for teachers comes in knowing how to use magnetic letters to create a memorable and effective experience for kids who might otherwise never learn the code.

17

Catch a
Falling Reader by . . .

Writing Words FAST

Success comes when children spend time reading, writing, spelling, learning vocabulary, creating ideas, and expanding their knowledge.

—Richard Gentry

When we were learning to drive a car, we needed to remember to attend to each and every action, right? We all remember those first few times well! We consciously reminded ourselves to look up at the rearview mirror and to push up on the turn signal if we wanted to go right. We focused only on what to do next, and there was very little time to think of anything else. Each action required our complete and total attention, thus making it difficult to talk, listen, or even change radio stations! Fortunately, with practice, we outgrew the need to consciously think about every little action taken while driving. Now we can be popping in a CD, handing the baby a cookie, rolling down a window for the dog, and still perform every action necessary to continue driving, we hope! The truth is that practice and repetitive behavior produce automaticity so that the brain is free to attend to other things beyond the basics.

Such is the case for falling kids. They are so busy attending to every single action that they cannot focus on the processes needed to read and write successfully. For example, when struggling children are asked to write in a journal, the first thing they probably do is balk at this task. Why? Because it is difficult for them and they don't feel successful at it. The next thing they'll do, since they still have to do it, is to figure out the easiest way to get it over and done with. So they'll pick a sentence that is fairly easy and safe. They begin by examining their pencil and finally landing it on the page where they will stop to ask themselves, "Does the letter *t* go to the top line or bottom line?" Then they'll proceed to write the *h* and *e* for the word "the." This may take a while for some and especially if the teacher happens to say, "Did you start your sentence with an uppercase letter?" Now they have to go back and erase that little *t* even though the word "the" does not look right to them with an uppercase *T*. What's next? They tear their paper while erasing that *t* and then drop their pencil. Now they fix the *t* but can't remember which way to make a *b* for the word "boy." While that is going on in their head, they wriggle around in their chair and think to themselves, "What am I writing?" Meanwhile, many of their peers are working their second and third sentences in the stories they are engaged in writing. A classic scenario, no?

We have all seen and worked with kids who struggle like this. Without a strong base of sight words in their personal bank of writing vocabulary, these kids continue to struggle and to attend to each and every action at a painfully slow speed. They simply aren't able to focus on what they are writing because they are too busy trying to remember how to write! Writing words *fast* is one way to build a bank of words that are automatic and easily retrieved by the child. This practice can be done with individuals or with children in a small group setting.

Here are a few suggestions for writing words *fast*:

- Use white boards and fine line markers because they are the best tools for writing words *fast*.
- Choose words they know, to start with. This will build success and keep motivation levels high.
- Say "Today we're going to practice writing words *fast* so that we don't have to think about them too much."

- Say "Write the word 'the' fast." As kids are writing, the teacher is circulating from behind, helping those who may hesitate on certain letters. It may be necessary to give a verbal command for forming the letter. An example of this would be, "down, up, and around" for the letter *h*. You will then want to encourage the child to practice this a few times, followed by writing the word "the" fast.
- After completing that word, ask them to erase it fast. "Now write that word again fast!" "Now erase it fast."
- Say "Now let's write the word 'an' fast. Good! Under that word, write the word 'and,' then look up at me!" "Great! Now erase them both and write the word 'that.'"

It's important to keep this practice short, sweet, and fast-paced. The power comes in doing this often and in keeping success levels high. These goals are best achieved by moving the kids along so that responses become automatic and fluent. The more they do this, the faster they get! The results will shine through in their journal writing because they will no longer be focusing on how to write each and every word they want to use. Their brains can begin to attend to the message they are writing. After all, isn't that what writing is all about?

18

Catch a Falling Reader by . . .

Engaging Learners With an Overhead Projector

> *When you have only two pennies left in the world, buy a loaf of bread with one and a lily with the other.*
>
> —Chinese proverb

I f you have only a small pot of money for teaching tools, buy an overhead projector and some magnetic letters. Do not underestimate the power of an overhead projector. It holds a certain magic for kids and is especially useful for those who have short attention spans. The overhead projector provides a unique way of demonstrating things while engaging kids in a fun way. Let's face it—this is a cool machine! Use it to catch falling kids whenever possible.

Let's look at a few ways to integrate the overhead projector into our instructional approaches:

During Guided Reading (Small Group)

- Specific words can be selected from the text to work with during the lesson. This is done by placing magnetic letters on the overhead and manipulating them to spell the word as we say the word. A child can come up and add the ending sound, or you can scramble the word and have someone make it and remake it. Colored magnetic tiles or projector letters can reinforce onset and rhyme. For example, if you selected the word "stand," you could demonstrate the onset (*st*) using blue letter tiles and the rhyme (*and*) using red tiles. Then you could demonstrate how to use both to build other words (i.e., "stick," "stop," "brand," "strand").

- The overhead projector can be used to record students' predictions during the introduction of the book. Graphic organizers such as a web or Venn diagram are especially effective because you can use colored markers on the transparency. This allows you to make the visual more attractive and appealing to the eye.

- An overhead transparency can be used to set a purpose for reading. For example, you might write, "Read until you get to the part where we found out that _____."
When your readers reach that part of the story, the teacher then records responses on the line, saying each word aloud *as* it is written. This type of modeling is productive and necessary for falling readers because of their strong need to see what good writing looks like. Other purposeful statements that might be written on a transparency: "Read until you figure out _____." "Read until you find three things that make you think that this story is true. They are _____, _____, and _____." "Read until you discover . . . We discovered _____."

During Shared Reading (Whole Group)

- The overhead projector can be used to enlarge a piece of text, such as a poem or math word problems. With a highlighter, the teacher and students can highlight rhyming words, common chunks and endings within words, or basic sight words.

- In addition to a highlighter, an index card or fly swatter with a box cut out of the center can be effectively used to find words within poems or chunks within words. Students also *love* to use the "magic paddle." It is simply a table tennis paddle or big spatula and is used to pull a word off the screen when it's projected. You might say, "Who can come up and use the magic paddle to pull the word 'stand' off the screen? Good. Now take the paddle and show me just the 'and' chunk in that word." This gives working with words a whole new, fun meaning for kids.

During Interactive Writing (Small Group)

- You will discover that falling readers often have difficulty writing their letter formations. An overhead projector can be useful for practicing letters over and over again. With a marker, children can trace your dotted letter right on the transparency. This is fun for children because they can actually see their letter up on the screen. It is also effective in helping children write that letter smoothly and automatically. The marker and transparency create a smooth flow that pencil and paper don't.

- For readers who need more work on hearing sounds in words (phoneme segmentation), an overhead projector can offer a nice change from the same old white board! The teacher would select a word with three or four sounds (e.g., "box," "hat," "swim," "drop"). With a marker, the teacher draws three (or four) connected boxes on the overhead transparency. Now place the magnetic letters for that word just below each box and demonstrate how to push each letter into the box *as* it is pronounced. You will then want to have kids come up to push and say the letters within each word. The visual demonstration of these enlarged letters in boxes on a big screen is powerful and can catch the attention of struggling learners. Don't have an overhead projector? Get one . . . now!

19

Catch a
Falling Reader by . . .

Encouraging
Repeated Readings

Although gold dust is precious, when it gets in your eyes, it obstructs your vision.

—Hsi-Tang

What is perhaps the most common characteristic of falling readers when they read aloud? It's word-by-word reading, or what I refer to as painful reading. The reader slowly plods along, focusing on individual words rather than on the flow of the text. In some cases, the reading is so slow and labored that we find it impossible to expect any comprehension to have occurred. In other words, the child is so focused on decoding and pronouncing the words correctly that the process of reading to gain meaning from print is obstructed. This is a problem for many falling kids.

One way to address this issue is to provide daily opportunities for children to read and reread in order to build fluency. Fluency occurs when words are read "like we talk," and this ability increases understanding. Specifically, if you increase fluency, you increase your chances for greater comprehension and success. Fluency, however, should not be confused with expression, intonation, and punctuation. Certainly those factors play a role in creating meaning as we read, but you can have readers who read with a monotone voice, yet they are fluent. Their ability to read the flow of the text accurately aligns with their ability to understand what is read, even if the tone of their voice is expressionless. This is rare, but it does happen among children.

If research proves that repeated reading increases fluency, then why don't we engage kids in this practice consistently? Good question! Perhaps a lack of time is preventing this from happening. With so many academic demands and constant interruptions throughout the short school day, it's a wonder that we teach to read with kids at all! However, that doesn't change the fact that we must make reading and rereading a priority, especially for falling readers who continue to read painfully and slowly. Rereading must be scheduled into their day in order to steadily increase reading speed and comprehension.

Here are a few suggestions for motivating kids to reread on a daily basis:

- Allow children to choose what *they* would like to reread. There's nothing more frustrating than working hard on a text and having someone say, "Good! Now reread that and it will be easier!" Children finally get through a difficult task and now they have to do it all over again? No way! When given choices between three and five different texts that the child has read before, it becomes less of a chore and more of an enjoyable event. Why? Because everyone likes to have choices!
- During guided reading, you can vary the ways in which you ask children to reread. For example, you can use a Reader's Theater format to teach expression, intonation, and fluent phrasing. You can also engage students in the "I'll read a page, you read a page" activity. When you read a page to children, you are modeling for them. This, ultimately, sets an example for the reader, and you will immediately notice an increase in their fluency when they try their page. If you don't believe me, try it!

- Asking children to read into an audio recorder is a powerful and fun way to get kids to reread. If you give them a bell, they can ring it when it's time to turn a page. They can then give the book and recording to the preschool or kindergarten children to follow along.
- Falling readers will benefit from rereading their writing often. They can do this by going back in their journals and selecting three or four entries to read to you or a friend. They may even find errors to fix as they reread.
- Don't be afraid to let students take the basal texts or reading series anthologies off the shelves so that they can reread stories that were read in small group lessons. Too many people are concerned that kids might read ahead and spoil the upcoming lessons. *Who cares!!!* Let them read whatever they will read whenever they can read it! Try getting some anthologies from earlier grades and letting kids read from those. They'll be easy as pie but highly effective for reinforcing earlier sight words and skills, for building motivation, and for making falling readers feel like they are progressing.

I don't think I need to repeat my thoughts on why it is important for kids to reread! So, let the rereading begin.

20

Catch a
Falling Reader by . . .

Establishing and Supporting a Daily Block of Reading Time

> *There is more treasure in books than in all of the pirate's loot on Treasure Island. . . . And best of all, you can enjoy these riches every day of your life.*
>
> —Walt Disney

With all that we know about the value of exercise and fresh air, have you ever wondered why every person on the earth doesn't take a 10-minute walk every day? The same is true for children and reading. If we know that practice is essential to anything and everything we learn, then why is it that we can't find at least 10 minutes per school day to allow children to read? So often I hear excuses such as bus evacuation drills, assemblies, field trips, eye and ear checks, and even lice checks! These are all legitimate pulls at our instructional time, but *nothing* is more important than learning to read. Therefore, it must take priority over everything else. It's that simple . . . and yet it's not. Maintaining an uninterrupted, daily session of quiet reading takes discipline, support, and work.

There are several ways that teachers and parents can ensure that children are getting better at reading by reading. Just as you and I have a variety of things to read on our nightstand or magazine rack, children need a wide range of things too. Falling readers tend to pick books that are way too difficult for them, and so they make up words as they turn the pages. This is fine for feeling like a grown-up reader, but they must also read for real. They must practice the skills and strategies that we are teaching them using a variety of different types of texts.

Create an individual book box for each child. You can use a shoe box, detergent box, dishwashing tub, or any plastic tub that's strong and movable. Let the kids pick lots of things to read from a variety of classroom bins. You may want to consider stocking up on the following things:

- Fiction and nonfiction "little" books
- Comic books
- Phone books
- Menus
- AAA tour books
- Maps
- Travel agency brochures
- Catalogs
- Dictionaries and thesauruses
- How-to books
- I Spy books
- Encyclopedias
- Classic novels

Pick one day per week designated as Book Swap Day and have the children pick a certain number of things out of their box to swap with friends or with other things from classroom bins. You will also want to be sure to put some books in boxes that *you* want your students to read. You can identify these books with a colored sticker and tell students that these books are to be read first. After they practice on these, they may read whatever they want in their book boxes. It's also a good idea to include a writing journal in the book box. This way, if children run out of things to read, they can always open their journal and write about their favorite book, change an ending, or draw a poster advertising their favorite item in their box.

The main thing to remember is that kids, especially falling kids, need to practice what they are learning. They also need to know *why* you are devoting time to quiet reading every single day. When I ask children around the country why their teacher has them drop everything and read, many of them will tell me, "So she has time to correct papers and to meet with us at her desk." Clearly, these students have not been taught *why* they must read every single day. Quiet reading time is not a time for us to correct papers or meet with children. We must be sure that we teach kids the importance of daily practice in everything we learn to do in life.

21

Catch a
Falling Reader by . . .

Teaching Kids How to Use a Listening Center

Children who have been particularly successful language learners are surrounded by adults who create many opportunities for children to use language to think, problem-solve, and reflect on their learning.

—Carol A. Lyons

I magine if every single primary grade classroom in the United States had a working listening center with working headphones, working cassette or CD players, and a wide variety of books, tapes, and CDs to listen to. In this day and age, where children are choosing to be entertained at home by a host of machines, it is important that we provide daily opportunities for them to listen to stories. So many parents are pressed for time these days, and even with the best of intentions, there are days that go by when children are simply not read to. This causes a problem, especially for falling readers.

Let's consider the benefits of supporting an active, engaging listening center before we discuss the best ways to teach kids to use this center properly. Listening to a variety of books on CD will help readers

- Build vocabulary and extend concepts
- Improve visual scanning skills (left to right and return sweep to multiple-lined text)
- Understand what fluent phrasing sounds like
- Use expression and intonation when reading as modeled in the stories they listen to
- Improve sight word recognition
- Attend to a variety of punctuation through modeling
- Broaden the range of topics and genre that students are exposed to
- Enjoy a story without stopping!

If a listening center is going to work in your classroom, it is important that you take some time to actually teach kids what you expect them to do and not do! When expectations are unclear, students tend to use the listening center as a time to fool around. By this I mean that they turn pages whenever they want to, chat with other kids while they're listening to a story, sweep across the lines in an effort to be done with the page, switch books and CDs midway through, play with the buttons on the recorder, adjust the headphones a million times, and any number of other behaviors that you can think of.

Recommendations for helping kids make the most out of a listening center are as follows:

1. Explain the purpose for the center and what you want kids to know and be able to do as a result.

2. Teach them how to properly insert a CD and how to work the player. They will need to practice this often with feedback from you.

3. Demonstrate how to go about selecting a story and CD. Then show them how to point to words *as* the recorded reader is reading. You will want to be sure that they understand

how to return sweep on multiple-lined text and that they know *when* to turn the page.

4. Show them how to put away the equipment and materials properly. They will need to practice this often with feedback from you.

5. It is recommended that three or four response sheets be available at the listening center. Children select a response sheet to complete after they listen to a book and CD. These response sheets can be graphic organizers (e.g., a web, Venn diagrams, story frames), or they can require a creative or artistic response (e.g., poster advertising the book, diorama of the story, new cover drawing, character puppets). Be sure to change the response sheets every few weeks so that students remain motivated to respond to each book and CD that they listen to.

22

Catch a
Falling Reader by . . .

Building Fluency in a Variety of Ways

Reading fluency refers to the ability of readers to read quickly, effortlessly, and efficiently with good, meaningful expression. It means much more than mere accuracy in reading.

—Timothy V. Rasinski

Have you ever considered why so many adults attend speed reading classes? There are lots of programs designed to assist adults in reading faster, but *why* do people spend their time and money on these? The main reason is comprehension. They want to understand what they read in less time than it currently takes them. Adult readers who have difficulty comprehending what they read usually read slowly. They were most probably falling readers who were able to read, but their reading rate was slow and labored. Attention was focused solely on the code or the visual cueing system, in many cases. These readers might have had so much trouble decoding that they ignored grammar and meaning cues in favor of isolated sounds, letters, and sight words. The result of this tedious journey leads to slower reading rates and, ultimately, comprehension problems. Fluency and comprehension are linked. One feeds the other.

When working with falling readers, we want to be sure that we are constantly building fluency in their reading so that they can gain meaning quickly and easily. What good is processing a whole book if you can't understand what you read?! Here are a few suggestions when supporting struggling kids as they strive for fluent phrasing, strong visual scanning skills, expression, and of course, greater comprehension:

- Flash sight word phrases at falling readers *daily*. I published two sets of 50 *Sight-Word Phrases* (Hebert, 2003a, 2003b), and I am delighted that teachers are using these throughout the country. They will help to build automaticity of basic sight words, increase fluent phrasing, train the eyes to visually scan left to right quickly, and improve vocabulary.
- When a reader is reading painfully, that is, reading each and every word slowly, you can suggest the following: "I'll read a page (or a line), then you read a page (or a line)." This should not be done regularly, but it is a form of modeling that works.
- When first graders demonstrate control over voice and print or one-to-one correspondence in early text levels, you will want to encourage them to "read with their eyes" now. That means getting the pointer finger out of there. They can bring their finger up if they get stuck, skip lines, or need to physically break up a difficult word. However, pointing to every word and shaking the head when pronouncing each word must stop, or fluency will be hindered. Say, "Good readers read with their eyes. Let me see you try that. Good for you! You are sounding like a good reader!"
- Model fluent reading whenever you engage children in shared reading with a big book or when reading back a class story during shared writing experiences. Do not spend too much of the year pointing to each and every word with a pointer. If you want to use a pointer to keep the kids' place when reading together as a group, *scan* the text with the pointer rather than deliberately pointing to each word. This

is good modeling, and it will lead to greater understanding on the part of the kids. They will copy you.

- For very tough cases of children who continue to read word by word into second and third grade, you may want to cut a small 1″ × 2″ piece of oak tag or poster board. Use the card to push across the words as a child is reading. That means that they need to read it before you cover it. This, in itself, is forcing the eyes to scan across the text, but you are controlling how fast they do this. Don't do it every day, but once in a while it can improve fluency and remind children to scan rather than point with their eyes.

- Teach fluency, expression, diction, intonation, and poise by engaging small groups of children in Reader's Theater. It is effective in building fluency because it forces readers to keep their eyes on the text. Even if they memorize their lines, do not allow them to take their eyes off the text as they read aloud. The key to successful Reader's Theater approaches is coaching. We must *teach* children how to project, scan, and perform the story with expression. This does not come naturally to many children, especially falling kids. They will build confidence in this approach because it is fun, engaging, fast, rhythmic, and positive.

As teachers and parents, we want our children to be proficient readers, writers, and thinkers. We must, therefore, strive to teach children how to read and write fluently so that their brains can attend to comprehension.

After all, we do read to gain meaning from the print, don't we? We need to be proficient at decoding as well as comprehending. Fluency matters!

23

Catch a Falling Reader by . . .

Using Focus Sheets and Graphic Organizers to Link Writing to Reading

> *The ultimate goal of teaching is to promote an orchestration process. It is important to note that orchestration occurs at the point where old knowledge meets new knowledge.*
>
> —Linda J. Dorn and Carla Soffos

C onsider the possibilities that exist for falling readers when we link writing to reading for them. This doesn't happen naturally for many kids who struggle. The reading and writing connection *must* be made by those of us who work with them. Small group guided reading lessons should include reading, writing, thinking, and working with words. They should not be limited to reading a new story every day. This is an outdated view of reading instruction that is slowly changing due to current research findings.

How do we link writing to reading? Guided reading focus sheets and graphic organizers are powerful tools that should be integrated into small group or one-on-one lessons. If kids have nothing to write on during reading lessons, then how can we make the link for them?

This is a question that I have pondered for many years, because most courses in reading instruction do not include writing in the small group lesson. For years, I've wondered why this has been the norm. I suppose it has to do with time—so what else is new? We can, however, find simple ways of including writing in the reading lesson if we are convinced that the reading and writing connection will catch falling kids. I know it can and does make a difference.

There are lots of published response sheets, transparencies, and graphic organizers available to teachers today. You will want to match the right tool with the lesson by asking yourself, "How can I link a writing response to this reading lesson?" For example, if I am doing a guided reading lesson using a text that reinforces "cause and effect," I might incorporate a graphic organizer into the lesson. Each student would have a copy of it, and together we would brainstorm examples of cause-and-effect events throughout the story. As the kids are writing, I am circulating *behind* them, offering help and support as they write.

Another example of integrating the writing into the reading lesson might be with the use of a blank sheet of paper. After a brief discussion of the title, cover, and pictures in the book, I might ask students to write down what they would like to learn from reading this book. *As* they write, I am observing, supporting, and prompting them. I would also record their answers on a chart as they read them back to me. This provides a model for writing while also giving us ideas for postreading discussions. This scenario creates a powerful reading and writing connection while simultaneously setting a purpose for reading the story.

It is worth the time and money to get published response sheets for use during guided reading or intervention lessons. Teachers should not have to use precious time and energy creating their own response sheets to match each book they teach with. Be sure to check the resource sections of your reading program manuals for graphic organizers and ideas for writing. Also, the appendices of many professional texts often include reproducible sheets that can be integrated into the reading lesson.

Here are a few additional resources for you to consider:

- *Teaching Guided Reading With Transparencies* by G. Byers (2002). Huntington Beach, CA: Creative Teaching Press.
- *Kid Writing: A Systematic Approach to Phonics, Journals, & Writing Workshop* by E. Feldgus & I. Cardonick (1998). Bothell, WA: Wright Group.

24

Catch a
Falling Reader by . . .

Providing Engaging Learning Center Activities

*Live a balanced life—learn some and think some, and draw and
paint and sing and dance and play and work every day some.*

—Robert Fulgrum

D o you believe that we actually learn by doing? I would be surprised if you didn't! When we are learning something, it is important that we try it, do it again, do it a different way, apply it in different situations and at different times, and so on. If kids actually don't have a chance to do what we're teaching them, then their learning is one-dimensional. Pencil-and-paper activities are necessary and vital for becoming proficient readers and writers. However, I would argue that engaging learning center activities play an equally valuable role in a child's literacy development, especially in the lives of falling readers. All too frequently, these kids fall into the mode of not being able to go to center activities because they take too long to finish seat work. This should never be allowed. They are the ones who need center-based learning the most!

What do we want kids doing while we're teaching small groups of students to read, write, and think? What do we want the rest of the class doing? When reflecting on these questions, ask yourself what you would want to see kids doing if you were invisible during the language arts block of the day. I would want to see them reading, writing, listening, speaking, working with words, solving puzzles, building, practicing handwriting, solving mathematical problems, conducting research investigations, and working with reference materials. If you take each one of these areas and create a corps of creative learning centers, you will be giving kids the practice that they need to move forward in many ways.

Here are some examples of engaging activities that might be included in elementary learning centers:

1. **Reading**
   - Boxes or bins of things (a wide variety of things to read at all levels and in all genres)
   - Read around the room (kids use a pointer to read posters, charts, labels, stories, the word wall, and anything else they can find on the classroom walls)
   - Big books, plays, poetry (kids can highlight rhyming words or basic sight words; they can practice reading and performing these with each other)

2. **Writing**
   - Picture file (laminated pictures that will stimulate ideas for writing)
   - Mystery box (place an object in a box. Cut a circle out of one end of the box and cover it with felt. Kids will feel the object and try to guess what it is. Have them write three to five adjectives to describe the object. Then they need to guess and write what they think it is)
   - Story starters (write open-ended writing prompts on laminated strips and place in a basket. Example: "If I were invisible I would . . ." or "One day, I found a $1,000 bill, so I . . .)

- Dictionaries and thesauruses (kids need to practice using these in a variety of ways)
- Different pens (provide a variety of different pens, pencils, fine line markers, and colored pencils for kids to explore in the writing center. We all have a favorite pen. So do kids!)
- Wordless books (a variety of different wordless books to stimulate ideas and to give kids a framework for writing a story to go with the pictures)

3. Listening

- Listening center (every classroom should have a good, working listening center for kids to listen to books and CDs on audio players. A variety of books and CDs are needed in order for this center to be engaging and motivating)
- Response sheets (after listening to a book and CDs, kids will choose from three or four boxes of creative response sheets, graphic organizers, or artistic activities in order to dive more deeply into the story they just listened to)

4. Building and Puzzles

- Legos, blocks, toothpicks, Q-tips, pipe cleaners (what can they build out of these? Put a different item out each week and watch them create!)
- Puzzles (how can you help kids attend to details, study the pictures, work collaboratively, and expand their attention? Puzzles!)

5. Science, Social Studies, and Research

- Nonfiction science and social studies books provide a variety of graphic organizers (e.g., webs, Venn diagrams, cause and effect tables, KWL charts (what they want to *know*, what they *already* know, what they learned) for use in exploring a variety of topics)
- Never-ending books (assemble a big book by using 10 to 15 sheets of oak tag or poster board and big rings to link them together. Teach kids how to look through nonfiction books for factual information. Then they each open to a clean page in the never-ending book and write at least two facts that they find about the subject the class is studying. Below the facts, they draw a picture or diagram

to support their findings. Never-ending books can be placed in the reading center when completed. A new book is used for each science or social studies area of study)

- Phone books (after teaching kids how to use the white and yellow pages of the phone book, display two posters on the wall above this center. On white poster board, list names of people for kids to look up in the white pages of the phone book. They need to use the guide words and record the page and phone number of that person. On the yellow poster board, list examples of things that kids would need to identify and look up in the yellow pages, for example, "You need a cab to the airport, your toilet is broken, or you have bugs in your house. Where will you look and who should you call?"

6. **Math**
- Quizmo, Bingo, Concentration, Checkers (all of these games are useful for practice with mathematics and reasoning. You can adopt these to include a wide range of addition, subtraction, multiplication, division, telling time, word problem words, etc.)
- Flash cards (we all learned the math facts with flash cards! Offer a variety of activities for kids to become automatic with basic math facts using flash cards)
- Pocket chart word problems (you can purchase or make math word problem cards that will fit in a pocket chart. Kids will manipulate the number cards within the problem and solve the problem in their math logs)

25

Catch a Falling Reader by . . .

Interacting With Kids as They Write

> *Discovery learning is the wrong approach to instruction; the case in favor of teaching as scaffolding is much more conceptually compelling, occurring as it does in the evening, when the Little Leaguer is fortunate enough to have an excellent baseball coach, and during the day, if the Little Leaguer is lucky enough to be enrolled in a classroom headed by an effective literacy teacher.*
>
> —Michael Pressley

F alling readers are falling writers. You will never find a child who can write well but can't read well. Therefore, if they struggle with reading, they struggle with writing. These learners cannot be allowed to merely discover writing behaviors, spelling patterns, decoding strategies, or sentence structure. They can and should be encouraged to write creatively in a journal and at a writing center, but the actual teaching of writing as they write is crucial. If you really think about it, when was the last time you were told to "take writing groups"? We have always been trained to take some groups of students for reading, but writing has predominantly been left to "go and write, then I will give you feedback." This is fine for kids who are progressing without much difficulty, but it is not enough for falling kids.

In a small group setting, consider the following suggestions for interacting with struggling kids *as* they write:

- Give each child a journal that has a top page and a bottom page and is bound together in the middle. The bottom page is for the child to write a message or short story. The top page is for the teacher to teach on! You will want to use this page to have them practice confusing letter formations, unknown sight words, new words, and any other things you can think of to help them write their story. The top page is for directing children to practice what is apparently difficult as you observe when they are writing.

- The key to interacting with kids *as* they write is to jump in and fix things quickly. For example, as you walk around behind the kids in the small group, you will notice when they get stuck. Let's suppose a child is trying to write "for" but he writes "far." You will want to take his pen and say, "What's a little chunk you hear in the word 'for'? Now write the chunk 'or' on the top page for me. Good, now under that write 'for.' Circle the little chunk you see in 'for.' So when you think of writing 'for,' you will listen for the 'or' and add an *f* in front of it! Now, before you fix it in your story, write the word 'for' in each corner of this top page *fast!*"

- You can and should also use analogies to help kids reach conclusions about the way words work. For example, if the child asks you how to spell "could," you will want to take the pen and on the top page say, "This word is 'would,' and this word is 'should.' Now circle what is the chunk you see that is the same in both of these words. Take my pen and circle that chunk in each of the words. Good, now if this is 'would' and this is 'should,' show me how you would write 'could.' Now practice that word three times before you write it in your story. That's a word you need to know by heart!"

- Using white correction tape is effective for covering up errors and helping kids fix their misunderstandings.

- Watch for behaviors that are missing from the brains of these kids. Two behaviors that are necessary for writing with ease are (1) saying a word out loud, slowly, as you write it, and (2) tapping difficult or long words as you say them aloud. These two behaviors are often foreign to falling readers and writers. They need to be taught to use these strategies to help them write new and difficult words. Otherwise, they resort to writing only the words that they know by heart. That's why many falling kids like to write "I like my Mom" or "I love my family" stories.

The teachable moment is the key to effective writing instruction for struggling kids. If we don't provide opportunities to teach them *as* they write, then we miss these fleeting moments. The goal is to help kids become independent, competent writers and readers. If we strive to give them enough strategies, fluency, writing vocabulary, ideas, confidence, and support while writing, they will begin to take off in their journey to reading and writing. Do not assume that they know what to do when they write. Many of them don't!

26

Catch a
Falling Reader by . . .

Providing Daily
Read-Alouds

Not to let the method get in the way of teaching,
Not to let teaching get in the way of learning,
But to send your knowledge of what must be learned
Out to meet the child's questions,
That is skillful teaching.

—Marie M. Clay

When we read to children, we teach them to use language as a means of communicating thoughts and ideas through the written word. We model what fluent reading "sounds" like. We introduce vocabulary that might otherwise be left unexposed to many students. We excite imaginations and stimulate creative thinking. We increase attention span and stretch listening skills. We encourage children to ask questions in our search for answers through a variety of print sources. Reading aloud is an essential approach to catching not only falling readers but all readers!

Reading aloud to students is not as easy as one might think. It requires thought, planning, and practice. What doesn't?! Before engaging in reading aloud to students of all ages, we would be wise to give some thought to the type of book we want to share each day, the purpose for selecting it as a read-aloud book, and the amount of time for each read-aloud session. Without prior thought and planning, the tendency is to just pick a book off the shelf and start reading. There is so much more to it! Reading aloud to students requires skillful teaching.

Here are a few questions to ask yourself as you prepare for reading aloud to children on a daily basis:

- What type of genre do I want to focus on today? Have my students been exposed to different types of poetry, informational text, and a wide variety of literature? Do I need to search for books in order to have a varied selection, or am I well stocked with books of all genres?
- Have I read the book that I selected to myself first? If not, why not? It makes all the difference in the world to "know your book" before sharing it.
- How long do I have to read to students today, and where are some juicy stopping points in the book? Juicy stopping points leave kids wanting more!
- How will I hold this particular book when I read it? Will I rest it in one hand, showing all the pictures to students as I read it? Will I switch hands occasionally, thus offering a different view of the pictures? Should I show some of the pictures *after* I read instead of *while* I read, building imagination and visualization skills?
- What is my purpose for reading this book to my students? Do they know my purpose? If not, why not?
- Can I extend their thinking of the story by modeling my own thinking? How can I model "interaction" with this book so that students will learn from my example? In what ways can I use this book to show evidence from the text after I read it, justifying answers to questions that lead to critical thinking? Do I want to read it solely for enjoyment, or do I have other intentions for using this particular book?

In the case of falling readers, we will want to read to them as often as possible. Many of these students have not been read to on a daily basis during preschool years, or many of them have simply not been exposed to good-quality literature. It has been my experience that teachers want and need recommendations for books that "must" be read to elementary students of all ages. Here are just a few of many that I personally recommend to teachers because they are all books that teach life lessons and provide opportunities to think, grow, and learn. In essence, they are classic, timeless stories.

- *The Little House* by Virginia Lee Burton (1978). New York: Houghton Mifflin.
- *Fantastic Mr. Fox* by Roald Dahl (1998). New York: Puffin Books.
- *Sylvester & the Magic Pebble* by William Steig (1969). New York: Simon & Schuster.
- *Babushka's Doll* by Patricia Polacco (1999). New York: Simon & Schuster.
- *A House Is a House for Me* by Mary Ann Hoberman (1982). New York: Puffin Books.
- *Blueberries for Sal* by Robert McCloskey (1948). New York: Viking.
- *The Little Yellow Chicken* by Joy Cowley (1996). Bothell, WA: Wright Group.
- *Hats for Sale* by Esphyr Slobodkina (1987). New York: William R. Scott.
- *Mouse Tales* by Arnold Lobel (1978). New York: HarperCollins.
- *Go Dog Go* by P. D. Eastman (1989). New York: Random House.
- *The Napping House* by Audrey & Don Wood (2004). Orlando, FL: Harcourt.
- *Two Bad Ants* by Chris Van Allsburg (1988). New York: Houghton Mifflin.
- *The Remarkable Farkle McBride* by John Lithgow (2003). New York: Simon & Schuster.
- *The Man Who Walked Between the Towers* by Mordicai Gerstein (2007). New York: Square Fish.

- *Fly by Night* by June Crebbin (1995). London: Walker Books.
- *Owl Moon* by Jane Yolen (1987). New York: Penguin Putnam Books.
- *Thank You, Mr. Falker* by Patricia Polacco (2001). New York: Penguin Putnam Books.
- *Sophie's Masterpiece* by Eileen Spinelli (2004). New York: Simon & Schuster.
- *The Mitten* by Jan Brett (1989). New York: Penguin Putnam Books.
- *The Heart of the Wood* by Marguerite W. Davol (1992). New York: Simon & Schuster.
- *Legend of the Indian Paintbrush* by Tomie dePaolo (1996). New York: Putnam & Grosset Group.
- *The Day of Ahmed's Secret* by Florence Parry Heide & Judith Heide Gilliland (1997). New York: Puffin Books.
- *The Very Quiet Cricket* by Eric Carle (1990). New York: Philomel.
- *The Giving Tree* by Shel Silverstein (1964). New York: Harper Collins.
- *Wolf* by Becky Bloom (1999). New York: Orchard Books/ Grolier.
- *Stellaluna* by Janel Cannon (1999). Orlando, FL: Harcourt.
- *The Children's Book of Heroes,* edited by William J. Bennett (1997). New York: Simon & Schuster.
- *Brother Eagle, Sister Sky: A Message From Chief Seattle* by Chief Seattle. (1993). New York: Puffin Books.

Part III

Reflection Promotes Action

Teaching is a craft. It never stays the same, nor does it die. It can only grow and change with time, effort, and practice. Educational leaders would be wise to value time for reflecting, sharing, debating, and thinking. One wonders what would happen if we are caught at our desks simply thinking about what we do and why we do it! Becoming a great teacher requires reflection. Reflection promotes action, and action leads to success. If we truly want to evolve into the kind of teacher who seems to "effortlessly" differentiate instruction for all learners, who makes connections for students, who produces independent readers, writers, and thinkers, and who has the ability to catch a falling reader, then we must set aside time to reflect on our practice. This section is intended to give the reader reasons to simply think.

Catch a Falling Reader by . . . *Seeking Balance Among "Best Practices"*
Catch a Falling Reader by . . . *Knowing What Each Child Needs*
Catch a Falling Reader by . . . *Observing What Good Readers Do*
Catch a Falling Reader by . . . *Breaking the Six Habits of Falling Readers*
Catch a Falling Reader by . . . *Creating an Assessment Table*
Catch a Falling Reader by . . . *Becoming Proficient at Taking and Using Running Records*

Catch a Falling Reader by . . . *Maintaining a Parent/Teacher Journal*
Catch a Falling Reader by . . . *Conducting Monthly Writing Sprees*
Catch a Falling Reader by . . . *Matching the Right Books to the Right Reader*
Catch a Falling Reader by . . . *Identifying Support and Challenges Within Books*
Catch a Falling Reader by . . . *Gradually Releasing Responsibility to the Learner*
Catch a Falling Reader by . . . *Reflecting on the Way We Do Things*
Catch a Falling Reader by . . . *Being an Energized Teacher*
Catch a Falling Reader by . . . *Becoming a "Starfish Flinger"*

27

Catch a
Falling Reader by . . .

Seeking Balance Among "Best Practices"

> *The only reason for time is so that everything doesn't happen at once.*
>
> —Albert Einstein

I f you were in an interview and asked to define "balanced literacy," what would your answer be? It is amazing how many definitions there are in the world for the same educational terms! The simplest and best answer to that question is based on the work of Margaret Mooney (1990) in her enlightening book *Reading to, With, and by Children*. Balance is the key, and yet we all struggle to provide this within the confines of the school day. Mooney sets a framework for defining balanced literacy in a simple but powerful way. It means that teaching and learning occur in the following ways:

Talking to kids
Talking with kids
Talking by kids

Reading to kids
Reading with kids
Reading by kids

Writing to kids
Writing with kids
Writing by kids

Although easy to define, it's not easy to do, right? The framework is only as good as our ability to do all of this *every single day*. This means that we are doing this all day long with all kids and all subject areas. It's essential that we balance each area, or there will be gaps in our kids' development and progress. Let's examine why this is so critical, especially with kids who begin to fall:

- If we leave out talking to, reading to, and writing to kids, we leave out the *modeling*. We learn from watching what others do well!
- If we leave out talking with, reading with, and writing with kids, we leave out the actual *instruction*. This means that a variety of whole group and small group instruction is needed to meet the needs of all kids.
- If we leave out talking by, reading by, and writing by kids, we leave out the *practice*. How can you learn to play an instrument or ride a bike without the practice?

So we have this framework of balls in the air. The tricky part is getting it all in every day, and this is where the frustration comes in for many teachers.

How can we do it all in the short time we have? Good question! I ask you to consider this analogy for a moment: Why is it that, even though we are given 24 hours each and every day, most of us cannot take a 10-minute walk daily?

Priorities must be established and maintained. Try cutting down on instructional time in each area so that you can get it all in. Try integrating subject areas more often. For instance, in order for children to become proficient at solving math work problems, they need to talk about them, learn how to read and comprehend them, and solve them with mathematical applications. Why not use math word problems for guided reading and shared writing experiences?

Remember that it's not the quantity of time we spend with kids, it's the quality of the time we have with them. We all wish we had more time to do it all, but is it really more time we need or better balance within the time we're given? All kids need balanced literacy so that they can become proficient, lifelong readers, but falling readers must have it if they are to move forward.

Don't forget to take a 10-minute walk today!

28

Catch a
Falling Reader by . . .

Knowing What
Each Child Needs

Start where the learner is.

—John Dewey

If you walk into any coffee shop on any given morning, this is what you will hear: "Regular with three sugars, no milk" or "Decaf with lots of cream and two sugars" or "Hazelnut with milk, not cream, and four sugars." These are typical orders of people who know what they want and what they need. Interestingly, there is usually little hesitation or uncertainty in the voices of those who order a daily cup of java. Even more fascinating is the fact that one rarely ever hears two orders that are exactly the same.

As I reflected on this silly but thought-provoking phenomenon, I thought, Wouldn't it be wonderful if every teacher and parent could order up exactly what kids needed so they could be caught and taught before it is too late? Of course it would be!

A sense of urgency can and should be created when a reader starts to fall. We become increasingly aware of our children's frustration levels, dependencies, and behaviors for coping with what is already too difficult. At the same time, we know that one program or method doesn't work for all children. So, the greatest challenge for teachers and parents comes in knowing what the child needs, when the child needs it, and which course of action to take.

Great educators have always known the power of ongoing assessment. As teachers, we would be wise to value the wisdom and research of those who came before us in the field. If we truly want to *know* children so we can catch them, we must assess performance on a regular basis, prescribe the best course available, and then *take action.*

Remember that planning and teaching are only as good as our ability to assess and reflect on the results. This leads to knowing where the child is so we can begin to move forward from there. The ultimate goal is to be able to target individual needs with clarity, certainty, and confidence.

The next time you go into a coffee shop, listen to those around you. They know what they want. Do you know what you want to order for each and every child who crosses your path? Figuring out what falling readers can do and what they need is hard work. Observation, assessment, and reflection can make the job a bit easier.

Now, go have a cup of coffee!

29

Catch a
Falling Reader by . . .

Observing What
Good Readers Do

In seeking wisdom, the first step is silence, the second listening, the third remembering, the fourth practicing, the fifth—teaching others.

—Ibn Gabirol, poet and philosopher

In the quest to catch every falling reader who crosses our path, we would be wise to stop and observe what good readers do. After all, we learn best from those who succeed, don't we? What do healthy eaters do to maintain weight control? How do good doctors prescribe the best medications? What do the greatest world leaders have in common? If we develop a solid understanding of what good readers and writers do at various stages in their literacy development, we can become better at knowing what may or may not be happening in the head of a struggling child. Easier said than done!

We can learn much from actually listening to the way good readers *sound* when they read. Notice how they problem solve new and unfamiliar words. Watch for different strategies and behaviors that they use when they first encounter a book or when they respond to questions. Observe the way they handle different types of books. Take note of what their eyes and fingers do when they encounter challenges as they read. Reflect on different ways that the reader uses different cueing systems to solve different print problems. This knowledge increases your awareness of what struggling readers are *not* doing. Awareness is half the battle!

Now, what do we do about it?

- Review and copy the following reproducible list of observable strategies and behaviors for each student you will be observing. It's a good idea to have a "clean" checklist for each book you ask the student to read.
- Choose several readers who are not struggling to read text at their grade level. You will want to hear each student in a quiet place, one on one. Competent readers are usually happy to show you what they know! This should be a relaxing, nonthreatening situation for each student.
- Tell the reader the title and offer a brief introduction of what this book is about. Explain that you want to hear the student (a) read the story or text aloud, (b) briefly retell the story when done, and (c) answer a few questions at the end.
- While the student is reading, highlight the items that best describe or summarize what you observe. It is valuable to do this with two or three fluent readers, each with two or three different types of texts (e.g., fiction, nonfiction, poetry, informational article, math word problems).
- As you reflect on the results, note behaviors that appear to be consistent and recurrent. Identify strategies that were applied to *all* types of texts and others that were used only with certain texts. Reflect on the comprehension skills and the ability to retell what has been read. This valuable information will confirm what you already know about good readers and sharpen your awareness of what good readers do with a variety of text levels and genre.

Reader Behaviors Checklist

(may be reproduced for classroom use only)

Child's Name: _____   Grade: _____   Date: _____

Title of Book: _____   Book Level: _____

1. Discusses the book title and cover, making inferences about the main idea of the story

2. Draws meaning from pictures and makes verbal predictions about what is happening in the story

3. Handles the pages of the book with ease, confidence, and independence

4. Shows control over left-right and top-down directionality

5. Demonstrates mastery of voice and print match by reading without adding or deleting words along the way

6. Keeps eyes focused on the text and/or pictures. Reader does not look up when encountering new and difficult words

7. Uses beginning and ending sounds, often articulating the first sound or sounds in new and unfamiliar words

8. Recognizes basic sight words easily and automatically

9. Uses eyes (not finger) to scan across lines of text and to return sweep on subsequent lines

10. Applies known chunks, syllables, and common endings to new and difficult words

11. Attends to punctuation marks appropriately in an attempt to gain meaning

12. Reads fluently, putting words and phrases together to sound like talking

13. Retells, infers, and evaluates what is read at a variety of critical thinking levels

14. Asks questions that lead to greater understanding

15. Cross-checks multiple sources of information and self-corrects independently, drawing on a combination of sources

Other observable behaviors and strategies:

_____

_____

_____

_____

_____

_____

_____

_____

_____

_____

_____

_____

_____

_____

_____

_____

_____

_____

Author's Note: It is important that teachers and tutors become proficient at taking and analyzing running records. It is also essential that students' writing samples be obtained and analyzed in order to gain greater perspective on problem areas that may be occurring in the reading.

30

Catch a
Falling Reader by . . .

Breaking the Six Habits of Falling Readers

Seek first to understand, then to be understood.

—Stephen Covey

What are six reading behaviors that have become habits among falling readers? Why do we need to be aware of them? How can we help children break these habits so that they can move forward in their literacy development?

I began to raise these important questions after assessing and teaching hundreds of falling readers. I observed the variety of unusual ways in which they decode, comprehend, and respond to challenges in their books. I watched what they did with their eyes, lips, and fingers. I analyzed their behaviors as well as their substitutions for new and difficult words. What I discovered was that struggling kids commonly adopt coping behaviors to deal with what is too difficult or frustrating. If left unchecked, these behaviors often become habits. Habits, as we all know, are hard to break, and new strategies are even harder to put in place!

You may want to visualize these coping behaviors as red flags that signal problems with the way a child is trying to learn to read. With this in mind, the first step is to become *a careful observer* so that you can identify behaviors that may be, or already are, habits. The second step is to *make the child aware* of the habit and simultaneously *offer alternative strategies* for coping with the text. The third, and most important, step is to *be consistent* in finding ways to help the child to break the habit. Reminding the child one or two times will not do it! The verbal prompts that we use to break habits and instill new behaviors are important. By consistently using the same verbal prompts, you will ultimately lead the reader to more effective strategies. This leads to success, success increases confidence, and confidence moves the child forward in new ways.

So, what are the six most common habits of falling readers and what should we do about them?

Habit #1: Look Up and Wait

This is perhaps the most common behavior that many children adopt when they are learning to read. If the text is too difficult or when readers don't know what else to do, they simply look up from the page and wait for someone to rescue them. Over time, this behavior happens more frequently, and the child begins to depend on others to problem solve new and difficult words. It is important that teachers, particularly first-grade teachers, deal with this behavior as soon as possible. We do this by frequently reminding the child that looking up will not help. Then we should jump in with a verbal prompt that will promote an action from the reader.

Examples of verbal prompts are as follows (not necessarily in this order):

- "Did you make the first sound? Try it!"
- "Why did you stop?"
- "Did you remember to check the picture?"
- "Tell me what's happening in the story."
- "What part of that word do you know?"
- "Why are you looking up? That won't help you. What else can we do?"
- "Use your finger to break that word up. Now try it!"

With consistent and firm prompting during reading instruction, the child will come to realize that looking up and waiting just doesn't work because nothing happens!

Habit #2: Skip the Word

Many emerging readers are prompted to "skip the word" when they come to words that are new or difficult. The basic philosophy behind this strategy is that by reading ahead, they will ultimately figure out what is happening and gain meaning. This is often true, but the problem with allowing young readers to skip the word is that they don't automatically return to figure out the word!

Skipping the word is really a higher-level strategy that is mainly used once a reader moves toward reading proficiency. In other words, good readers at higher levels will sometimes skip a difficult or unfamiliar word, but they will always return to decode that word. Young readers who are taught to skip without working out the word begin to rely on this behavior as a way of coping with challenging words. Over time, the reader begins to skip many words, and this eventually backfires, because the text no longer makes sense when reading ahead.

Breaking this habit requires consistent teaching in phonetic decoding and the way words work. That is, children must be prompted and expected to check specific visual cues within a word instead of skipping and forgetting it. Verbal prompts include the following:

- "Let's take a look at that word you skipped. I didn't hear you make that first sound. Try it. That will help you."
- "Take your two pointer fingers and frame a little part you know in that word. Now try it."
- "What word would make sense there? Does it look right? Check it."
- Give the child three choices of possible words:
  Could it be _____? Could it be _____?
  Could it be _____? How do you know?

Skipping words is an easy out! Unless you're going to teach them *how* to go back and problem solve the new word, don't encourage skipping until they are more experienced readers.

Habit #3: Sounding Out Every L-e-t-t-e-r

We've all worked with readers who sounded out every letter when they came to a new or difficult word. This type of behavior focuses on distorting the sounds in a word rather than instantly recognizing it or decoding it. For example, children who resort to sounding out the word "would" might verbalize "w-o-uh-l-d." They could do this all day and never get the word! More important, the flow of the sentence and meaning of the text are lost due to the time it takes to stop and distort the word by individual letter sounds.

Why do falling readers resort to sounding out individual sounds within words?

Here are a few reasons:

- For years, someone has told young readers to "sound it out" when they read. That's what they've been told, so that's what they do.
- Readers don't know what else to do because effective strategies and skills have either not been introduced or they are being ignored by the reader. In the latter case, falling readers find it easier to stop and sound out because eventually someone will come to their rescue and tell them the word.
- These readers often ignore clues from the meaning and structural (grammatical) cueing systems, thus only relying on the visual (phonetic) system.
- Overemphasis on isolated phonics skills without a link to context was taught, in the early years, to the exclusion of processing strategies. These strategies include sight word recognition, searching pictures for meaning and inference, rereading the line when stuck, checking for grammatical sense, and identifying common chunks within words.

The sounding out habit is very hard to break, but it must be broken or readers will continue to struggle. This habit often stops the flow of the story. When this happens, there is little, if any, fluency, and this can limit comprehension.

So, what do we do about this habit?

1. Tell your struggling readers that sounding out every letter will not help. Say, "What can you do to help yourself?" If

they don't know, remind them of a few key strategies such as first sound, rereading, and looking for known chunks within the word.

2. Verbal prompts that you give to readers as they're reading are vitally important for breaking bad habits. Be sure to prompt readers to look for parts that they know in the word, search the pictures and check the first sound, look for common endings, break apart the word with their fingers, and so on. Your prompts should be consistent in their wording, and your voice must carry a sense of urgency so that the reader will engage in the action you are seeking.

3. Increase daily practice with sight words (while both reading and writing) so that a strong bank of frequently used words can be instantly recognized. This will increase confidence and free the students' attention for problem solving new and difficult words.

4. Add writing instruction (shared writing and interactive writing) to reading instruction time, in both small group and whole group settings.

The bottom line regarding the sounding out habit is not to tell young readers to sound out in the first place!

Habit #4: Guess the Word

Readers who guess at a word and go on to the next words are simply not checking on themselves. In technical terms, they have not learned to self-monitor and cross-check multiple sources of information. They may look at the word "winter" and say "water." They may frequently guess at words that start and end the same, but they fail to check medial sounds and meaning. They may get close to the meaning, however, so they accept their substitution and move on. An example of this would be when the reader says "shrieking" for "shouting." The beginning and ending sounds are similar. The guess is grammatically correct, and the reader is able to get a sense of the meaning. Early on, the reader learns merely to guess without checking to be sure the word is correct. This habit magnifies itself in upper grades, where guessing many words results in poor comprehension and the inability to recall details.

Here are a few suggestions for breaking the guessing habit:

- Don't let it get started in the first place! We all need to take risks at words when we're reading, but our brains tell us to check it for accuracy. Prompting early readers, as they are reading, will help to get them off on a good start. Verbal prompts might sound like this: "You said 'ground.' "Check it! What letter would you expect to see at the end of 'ground'? Were you right?" Make certain that your prompts include the phrase "Were you right?" This prompt needs to be firmly established in the head of a falling reader. Without it, they will simply guess and go on to the next word.
- When readers guess at a word, take their finger and show them how to look at a part in the word that will contradict the guess. For instance, if children read "shrieking" for the word "shouting," say, "I see a chunk, you know, in the middle of that word. Take your fingers and frame that chunk 'out.'" Then ask, "Can it be 'shrieking'? Try it again and look for parts in the middle of words."
- As they move into higher grades, readers no longer read out loud to themselves. They read internally. This is an important transition and one that usually happens naturally. However, it is important that we still hear children read aloud in order to check on fluency and accuracy. You can't be in the head of children while they're reading silently! But you can ask them to read aloud when you come behind them, and you can take frequent running records in order to determine whether guessing is a problem or not.

Habit #5: What's That Word?

Ah, now there's a line we've all heard a million times! Readers come to a word they don't know and shout, "What's that word?" Why is this question a problem that needs to be addressed? It is a signal that the reader is learning to depend on others to solve print problems. Every time children ask the question, they rely on someone else to give them a prompt, a clue, or the word. If done often, the question replaces good reading strategies and behaviors that will lead to independence. Remember, the idea is gradually to release responsibility to the reader. This is the heart and soul of our work with falling readers. They must not depend on others to simply tell them the word.

Easier said than done? You bet! So, what do we do about those kids who keep asking us what the word is?

1. Prompt the reader by saying, "What do you notice? What's that first sound? Try it! Go back and try it again. What can you try?" These are all verbal prompts that will encourage the child to take some sort of action. You may still decide to tell them the word, but not until you've given children a chance to take some action on their own. If done consistently, this will move the reader away from constantly asking you for the word. Consistency is the key word, however.

2. Be sure that you are matching the right books to the right readers. By this I mean that if readers are asked to apply strategies on text that is too difficult, they may simply give up. In the process of trying to read something that's frustrating, children have no other choice but to depend on you for the words. So they say, "What's that word?" each and every time they feel defeated. Proper book choice is a key to preventing this habit.

3. Readers who already rely heavily on this habit will need to back up to easier texts so that they feel successful with the strategies you are teaching. As you slowly increase the level of difficulty, you can prompt the child to try that word again or you can ask, "What can you do to help yourself?" This is, ultimately, what we want all readers to be saying when they come to new challenges in their texts, right?

Habit #6: Reading Word by Word

One might say that reading word by word, or what I call *painful reading*, might be merely a lack of fluent phrasing. You would be right to assume that, but what happens when this painful reading becomes the status quo? What happens when, to the child, it is the way they read and that's that? Now it's a habit, and we know how hard those are to break! So we need to move readers forward with fluency so that they don't get used to hearing themselves read word by word.

Why do many falling readers read this way? One theory is that they are encouraged to use their fingers to point to each and every word long after they need it. What is the pointer finger for anyway? In beginning readers, we encourage children to point to their words so that directionality and voice and print match will be firmly and consistently established. This means that while they're reading, they don't add any words, take away any words, skip any lines, or miss any pages. Once these early strategies are in place, however, readers need to begin to use their eyes to scan. Good readers move their eyes ahead as they read. Think about yourself as you are reading. Your eyes are never actually *on* the word you are reading. As proficient readers, we scan our eyes ahead, and this leads to fluency or putting our words together like we talk. Fluency increases our reading rate and, ultimately, our comprehension of the text.

So what do we do about word-by-word readers?

- Encourage the reader by saying, "Now read it with your eyes. You don't need your finger anymore!" Or you could also say, "Now try it again and use your eyes to read it like you talk."
- Once readers have established directionality and voice and print match or one-to-one correspondence, you can begin to flash sight word phrases daily. This will increase instant recognition of sight words while also building visual scanning and fluent phrasing skills. Tell your readers to read them fast and play games with phrases so that the task is fun and engaging (Hebert, 2003a, 2003b).
- When a child is reading word by word, you might say, "I'll read a page, you read a page." Just by hearing you read fluently, the child begins to imitate the way you sound. Modeling is extremely important, and it works like magic!
- Say, "Try that again, and this time, put your words together like you talk."
- Encourage fluent reading by engaging students in Reader's Theater. There are many books that lend themselves well to this approach. Simply assign parts and have the children perform the story with expression, fluency, rhythm, attention to punctuation, and good diction. I have the children turn their backs to the audience (or the teacher) so that

they stay on their toes when it's their turn to read. This also keeps the audience engaged. If done often, Reader's Theater is a wonderful way to build fluency, confidence, visual scanning skills, and a movement away from word-by-word reading. Try it!

If we truly want to catch every falling reader, then we must strive to be like doctors, observing and analyzing symptoms, prescribing antidotes for addressing these symptoms, and recommending preventive care for the future. This is a tall order, given the structure and organization of our schools. Ideally, we should be providing one-on-one, short-term intervention for each and every child who starts to fall. Bad habits are hard to break and even harder to stop, especially when a child's ability to read is at stake.

31

Catch a Falling Reader by . . .

Creating an Assessment Table

> *When they assess for learning, teachers use the classroom assessment process and the continuous flow of information about student achievement that it provides in order to advance, not merely check on, student learning.*

> —Richard Stiggins

W hat do we want kids to know and be able to do? How do we know they know it? What are we going to do about it? These are the most important questions we can ask ourselves.

Interestingly, the answers to all of these questions have something to do with how we assess kids and what we do with the results. Unfortunately, "assessment" is a loaded word in the field of education today. The term is used to refer to state assessments, local assessments, program assessments, textbook assessments, informal assessments, required assessments, optional assessments, and, oh yes, observation, evaluation, and recording results in between!

Here's a silly analogy to simplify the role of assessment: Have you ever baked a cake? If you have, you probably "assessed" the cake at some point by sticking a fork or toothpick into it to see if it's done. You would never think of ignoring the results of this informal assessment, would you? In other words, you wouldn't just report the status of your cake to your boss or spouse and then go shopping! You would *immediately take action*, and this action would be based on observation as well as the results of your assessment. If your fork had batter on it, you would set the timer for 10 more minutes and leave the cake in the oven. If, on the other hand, your fork had no batter on it and the cake looked done, you would take it out and turn the oven off.

How strange that so many school districts require assessments but merely ask teachers to report the scores! Where's the action that occurs as a result of these assessments? This is the ultimate question.

Consider what most of us spend the majority of our time doing as teachers. Planning, teaching, planning, teaching, planning, and teaching! Traditionally, assessment has occurred in ways that interrupt instruction. Imagine how often we could assess students on a regular basis if we utilized an assessment table in our classrooms. I know I would be much more likely to call children over in between activities to hear them read, write, and speak. If I assessed one child per day, I'd have a continuous flow of information to use when planning and teaching. Assessment data also assist us with grouping decisions, book choices, teaching tools, and parent conferences.

What's on this assessment table? You will want to create your table based on the literacy assessments that are required, essential, and optional at your particular grade level. There are some things, however, that could be considered for all assessment tables in the elementary grades. Here are just a few suggestions:

- A literacy folder for each child with a checklist of literacy skills and strategies stapled to the front of each folder
- A date stamp (for dating assessment data)
- Running record booklets and forms (copied and ready to use)
- A set of sight words along with a form for recording results

- A set of sight word phrases along with a form for recording results
- Several wordless books to check on oral language structures, prediction skills, word retrieval, and diction
- A 0.7 mechanical pencil with an eraser (best for recording running records)
- Writing paper, fine line markers, and several writing prompts or pictures for obtaining a writing sample
- Math flash cards along with a form to record results
- Informal spelling and phonics assessments
- Published reading inventories (for advanced and upper-elementary students)
- A white board or "magna-doodle" for observing letter formations, letter and sound sequences, and fine motor skills
- A few easy-level books for kids to warm up with
- Parent/teacher journal (if established)
- An interest inventory or questionnaire to determine kids' likes, dislikes, feelings, and confidence levels

Assessing one child each day can take the guesswork out of planning and teaching while also assisting us in differentiating instruction for individuals. Daily assessment of students helps us to know where we need to go, because we know what they can do and what they need. This is critically important for falling readers and writers.

So, stick that fork in your cake and then take action!

32

Catch a
Falling Reader by . . .

Becoming Proficient at Taking and Using Running Records

Other than an MRI, there is no greater way to get into the heads of kids than when they are reading.

—Connie R. Hebert

R unning records are not new to the world. They were designed and introduced to the field in the mid-1970s by Dr. Marie Clay, New Zealand educator, psychologist, and researcher. Teachers needed a way to observe, record, and analyze what children were doing as they were reading. This could only be done by actually sitting down beside children and hearing them read aloud. As the child is reading, the teacher records what the child is reading using a universal code. This code indicates the child's correct responses, errors, omissions, insertions, repetitions, substitutions, and a host of other behaviors.

The *only* way to become proficient at taking running records is to take them often. This means taking them *daily!* The more you do them, the better you get at using the code at the child's pace and text level. As with shorthand or typing, proficiency comes with practice, practice, and more practice. There are many professional books, self-tutoring CDs, seminars, and courses that offer training in doing running records. If you're not trained yet, you should complain to your undergraduate school of education and then find a way to receive this training.

Once you feel confident with taking running records, you can move into the analysis arena. This is the most important part of the process, as it allows you to plan and teach with the child's individual strengths and needs in mind. Running records can teach us many things about a child's reading skills and strategies, but there are four main things you will want to focus on as a classroom teacher:

1. What are the child's independent, instructional, and frustration reading levels? These are determined in percentages using the number of words in the book or passage that the child reads.

2. After determining the number of errors that the child made, what patterns can be determined for guiding your next move with this child? For example, is the child sounding out every letter on new or difficult words? If so, this reader may be relying solely on visual (or phonetic) clues while ignoring meaning and grammar.

3. How does the child sound when reading aloud? Do you hear fluent phrasing, similar to putting words together, or do you hear painful word-by-word reading?

4. Which comprehension strategies will be used after the oral reading of the text: retelling, questioning, graphic organizer, picture, or written response? How does comprehension align with the child's oral decoding strategies?

Without the use of running records on a regular basis, I am totally baffled as to how one can truly catch falling readers and advance them to new heights. Running records are worth our time and effort—become a running records pro!

33

Catch a Falling Reader by . . .

Maintaining a Parent/ Teacher Journal

When love and skill work together, expect a masterpiece.

—John Ruskin, author, art critic,
and social reformer

W hat a beautiful thought: love and skill working together! The need for parent involvement in literacy development has never been greater. This does not mean that parents should teach their kids to read or that they should be spending an hour each night helping their children with a difficult book. Most parents are not certified teachers, and they don't have the expertise to fix a falling reader. However, parents play a key role in the values placed on children. If you believe that reading is important, so will your child! If you believe that your child has the potential to be a great reader and writer, then your child will become what you want your child to become.

Reading to children every day is the single best way to keep motivation high and skills sharp. Falling readers also need daily opportunities to read *to* someone as well. They simply don't have enough time during the school day to practice what they are learning. Reading to someone can help them cement new strategies, reinforce sight vocabulary, build self-confidence, and improve comprehension skills.

Another important way that parents can stay actively involved in their child's literacy development is to establish a parent/teacher journal. This form of communication serves as a bridge between what is happening at home with what is happening at school. It can even take on a third dimension by including the child's intervention teacher. For example, falling readers who attend Title I or Reading Recovery lessons can benefit from input from the teachers of these programs as well. So, a parent/teacher journal connects the home, school, and intervention program in an effort to provide accelerated, consistent progress for children.

A daily journal is highly recommended, but if this is not possible, then perhaps the journal could go home on Fridays and return with parent comments every Monday morning. Here are a few considerations for making the most out of your parent/teacher journal.

Suggestions for Teachers and Intervention Specialists

1. Establish the journal as early in the year as possible. A good time to explain its purpose and use is during the fall parent conference. Be sure that parents understand the importance of maintaining the journal with a set schedule. They also need to know what you want them to comment on (see Suggestions for Parents below).

2. Explain that you value their feedback and insights about what is happening at home. You want to know if the child is feeling good about his or her progress with reading and writing. You want to know if the child is frustrated or unhappy in school. You also want to know how the child reacts to new and unfamiliar books that are sent home to read to someone. This is important information that can

help to accelerate a falling reader's progress. Make this clear to the parents. They play a key role, and they need to know that you welcome and appreciate their involvement. You will also want to help parents understand a few key points that they may not know already.

Go over the following list of strategies with parents. It will help parents when they are working with a falling reader at home:

- Encourage your child to use the pictures to gather meaning. Do *not* cover the pictures when your child is reading.
- Beginning readers use their pointer finger to help them match their voice to the print. This will not last long, but you will want to encourage pointing when they are first learning to read.
- If children are stuck on a word, parents can prompt them to help themselves by reminding them to make the first sound and try it again, to check the picture and reread the line, to look for a little part in the word that they know, or by giving them a few choices (e.g., "Could it be 'ground,' could it be 'green,' or could it be 'grass'? You check it."
- Read a "good" book to your child every night. Try to choose a variety of genre to read, for example, a fairy tale, fable, poem, toy catalog, map, recipe book, comic book, how-to book, I Spy book, dictionary.
- If children are reading a book from school and they are reading word by word with a slow, deliberate pace, suggest that you will read a page and they will read a page. This serves as a model for fluent reading and shows children how to put their words together like they talk.
- Above all, parents should build children's self-confidence as readers by pointing out specific things that they notice children are now doing. You can also leave notes or write on a white board outside your child's bedroom door. By communicating your thoughts in writing, the child learns to value writing and to see it as another form of expression. Whenever possible, have your child write, write, write!
- Get some magnetic letters for the refrigerator door. Have some fun every morning making and breaking words with your child. Children will show you lots of words they are learning in school. Build on those and praise your child for new discoveries along the way.

Suggestions for Parents

The parent/teacher journal is a bridge between the home and the school. Please take an active role in communicating with your child's teachers so that they can know how to serve your child better.

Here are a few things you may want to think about when responding in the journal:

- How does your child *feel* about himself or herself as a reader?
- Does your child bring books to you on his or her own, or do you need to remind your children each time you sit down together?
- Is your child able to discuss the cover and pictures in the book with you prior to reading?
- Does your child race to get through the book?
- What does your child do with words that are new or difficult?
- Is your child saying anything that the teacher should know (e.g., "These books are *way* too easy!" "I don't like reading group . . . it's boring." "When can I read harder books?" "Why do I have to do this at night?" "I feel dumb because the other kids read faster and harder books." "Why do I have to go to that 'other' teacher every day?" "I don't like to write in my journal . . . it's boring and hard."
- How does your child respond to you when asked questions about a story he or she just read or when you ask your child to retell a story you read together?
- What questions do *you* have for the teacher? Use the journal to help you understand your child's literacy progress. You don't have to wait for parent conferences to ask questions and get answers.

Communication between the home and the school is vitally important if we are going to catch falling kids. Yes, it requires time and effort on the part of parents and teachers, but kids are worth it! Get going!

34

Catch a
Falling Reader by . . .

Conducting Monthly Writing Sprees

Have patience! In time, even grass becomes milk.

—Charan Singh, mystic

What do we want kids to know and be able to do *fast?* We want them to be able to write basic sight words quickly and easily. The ability to do this frees them to attend to harder things when they write, such as sentence structure, new and multisyllabic words, concepts about print, punctuation, and creativity. When they have to think about how to write a single word, they stop thinking about the message they are writing and focus only on that word. What's even worse is when they forget how to write the letters of the word. Now they have to stop, figure out the letter, say the word, and try to write the word. All of this takes away from writing, and falling kids tend to quit.

What can we do about this? We can start by having kids write words *fast* on white boards with fine line markers every day. We can also gain a great sense of what words they know if we conduct monthly writing sprees with falling readers. The information gained from this informal assessment is extremely valuable to the teacher. It supplies the teacher with data about which words are cemented in the child's brains, how the child links words, the child's ability to hear sounds in words, and any handwriting issues.

Here are the steps for conducting monthly writing sprees:

1. Call children over to your assessment table by saying, "Come and show me all the words you can write now!"

2. Let the children pick a dark fine line marker to write with and offer a blank sheet of paper. Be sure the children are not sitting where they can see the word wall! Sit next to, not across from, the children. Sitting next to the children during assessment sends a message of support rather then one of checking up.

3. Set your timer for 10 minutes and ask the children to write as many words as they can *fast!* You probably won't need to prompt the children at first.

4. When the children hesitate or appear stuck, offer some prompts such as, "How about little words like 'at,' 'or,' 'is,' 'in,' 'the'?" "How about some color words?" "You wrote 'go' and 'stop.' Can you write 'going' or 'stopping?" "How about some animals like 'dog,' 'cat,' 'pig,' 'cow'?" "Now can you do 'cats,' 'dogs,' 'pigs'?"

5. You are trying to see how many words children can write off the top of their head. You want to keep children actively engaged and moving along. You can do this by creating a sense of urgency in your voice.

6. Give the children more blank paper if they fill up the first sheet. The main thing is to keep the process going for 10 full minutes and to get down as many words as the children can think of.

7. When done, you will want to count all the words that the children spelled correctly. You will be looking for any errors that are consistent such as short vowel sound confusions, trouble with blends or endings, letter formation and

spacing issues, and so on. You will also want to note the children's ability or inability to link, for example, if they wrote "at," "that," "the," "then," "there," "or," "for," "fort," "go," "going," "swim," "swimming." This is a window into their understanding of phonetic rules.

A more formal explanation of a writing vocabulary assessment can be found in Marie Clay's (1993) *An Observation Survey of Early Literacy Achievement*. A monthly writing spree can give you information about children's writing vocabulary, handwriting skills, uppercase and lowercase usage, sight vocabulary, and linking abilities. This is *not* a spelling test where you say a word and the child writes it. It is a chance for falling readers to show you what their bank of writing vocabulary is and to show off once a month. First graders who can write 45 to 50 words in 10 minutes by January of the school year are probably not falling kids. You will want to push your falling readers forward by doing a lot more writing so that they can reach that benchmark.

35

Catch a
Falling Reader by . . .

Matching the Right Books to the Right Reader

Using a variety of texts during guided reading is necessary to help students learn what it means to be a reader. Remember that we are teaching children to be readers rather than merely teaching them to read.

—Michael F. Opitz and Michael P. Ford

To catch a falling reader, we must know which books to use and which ones not to use. Matching the right books to the right reader requires skill, knowledge, and intuition. Although we need to know the books we have access to for guided reading groups and home use, we must also know our learners. Assessment and book choice are closely linked, and those who use this link have greater success rates with falling readers. Use your running record data to help you select the right book for the right reader. After catching hundreds of falling kids, I can promise you that the ability to move them forward depends significantly on your book choices for them. It is worth the time and effort.

Before selecting a book for instruction, ask yourself the following questions:

Too Easy

If I choose this text, will my readers

- Demonstrate the use of a variety of strategies needed to read this book independently?
- Be able to read most sight words in the book instantly?
- Grasp the concept or story line of the book with very little prompting?

Just Right

If I choose this text, will my readers

- Find some supports in the text that will help them feel somewhat successful?
- Encounter a few challenges that will give them opportunities to problem solve new and difficult words?
- Be able to work on fluent phrasing in order to increase comprehension at a variety of levels?

Too Hard

If I choose this text, will my readers

- Find the content and vocabulary beyond their prior knowledge and experiences?
- Struggle with every few words in this text?
- Feel successful when attempting this text for the very first time?
- Read it fluently or painfully?

Choosing the right books for the right readers takes time, patience, and perseverance. The more we can learn about proper book choice, the better we will all be in catching falling readers.

36

Catch a
Falling Reader by . . .

Identifying Support and Challenges Within Books

There's a mismatch between the needs of the student and what's being offered.

—Eric Jensen

When you plan a reading lesson, what do you ask yourself? I have to ask myself the following question and then be able to answer it *before* I teach the lesson: "What do I want kids to know and be able to do as readers, writers, and thinkers as a result of this lesson?" When I know the answer to this, then I can justify the reason for my book selection. Too often we select books for instruction because they are the "next story in the basal" or because "we are studying about that subject in social studies." These are supplemental reasons.

The main reason for choosing a book for guided reading instruction must be because of what the book can do to help you reach your outcome for these kids. The outcomes come from state standards, grade level benchmarks, and scope and sequence charts. Ongoing assessment will also give us information about which skills and strategies are needed. For example, if a group of struggling readers is still reading word by word slowly, then we would select several books that will promote fluent phrasing and meaningful context. These books or stories might also be linked to our social studies unit, but the main reason for choosing them for instruction is to build fluency skills for these particular readers.

One of the most helpful exercises for selecting books is based on a search for supports and challenges within books. Here's how to do it:

1. Select several books, stories, and paragraphs that you believe will help meet the outcomes for a particular student or group of students. Read each book from cover to cover! Don't skip any pages or any lines.

2. On a sheet of paper or an index card, make two columns: one with the heading Supports and the other with the heading Challenges.

3. Now consider the following characteristics before deciding which of them will be a challenge and which will be a support for the readers you will be teaching:
   - *Print:* layout, size, font, boldness, placement on each page
   - *Vocabulary:* frequency of sight words and unfamiliar words, single syllable versus multisyllabic words, repetition of certain words
   - *Pictures:* single items versus scenes, highly supportive or moderately supportive of texts.
   - *Punctuation:* simple punctuation (e.g., periods, question marks) versus a combination of punctuation marks (e.g., periods, commas, quotation marks, exclamation marks).
   - *Oral Versus Written Sentence Structure:* grammatical structure of the story written the way "kids talk" versus more advanced sentence structure commonly found in written text.
   - *Fiction Versus Nonfiction:* differences in concepts, meaning, and vocabulary.

4. After considering the above characteristics within the book, decide which of these features will be a support to the readers and which ones might challenge them. Some of the characteristics will not be applicable to the book that you've selected, but many of them are. For example, you might identify the print layout as a support because it is consistent (text on left and picture on right), and you might consider the number of lines on each page and the size of the font to be challenges. Only you can decide which characteristics are supports and which ones are challenges, because these decisions will be dependent upon the competencies and needs of the students for whom you are selecting the text. Daily practice with identifying supports and challenges within texts is really the only way to become competent and comfortable with this.

5. Once you've listed supports and challenges for a particular text, you are now ready to plan the lesson. You will not teach *to* these items, you will simply use the characteristics you've identified to prompt and guide your readers as they read this new book.

Identifying supports and challenges within books becomes easier if you do it often. It's even easier when you know your books by heart. This information will also help in selecting more books for your classroom and school's literacy closet. You will recognize levels that are missing key characteristics or are limited in their supports for struggling readers.

Spend time with your books. If you become proficient at selecting books that both support and challenge your falling readers, you will catch them much sooner than you think! Trust me.

37

Catch a
Falling Reader by . . .

Gradually Releasing Responsibility to the Learner

Few things can help an individual more than to place responsibility on him, and to let him know that you trust him.

—Booker T. Washington,
reformer, educator, and author

J ust catching falling readers is not enough. We must catch them, teach them, and guide them, with the ultimate goal being the gradual release of responsibility. Children who rely on adults or friends to help them with every task are creating dependencies that will not serve them well in the future. Unfortunately, there are those who do not believe in the tough love approach to teaching. In the case of struggling kids, there is no other way. They must be expected to fly or they won't! So many people see these kids as poor victims who are all too often labeled as delayed, disabled, slow, low, and so on. If you don't see these kids as victims, they won't be!

Each and every time we teach falling children a new skill, we must expect them to take it, use it, and run with it. Teacher expectation plays a huge role in the success or failure of falling kids. If you expect them to learn, they will. If you expect them to have trouble, they will! Remember, kids become what they think *you* want them to become! That's just the way it is. We would be wise to remember that as we relate to falling readers. Every day, the message must be that you *can* do this, you *will* do this, and I will help you until you can do this on your own. The goal of the teacher and parent should always be the gradual release of responsibility, because without that, the child is paralyzed to perform independently.

Move the train slowly for falling kids, but move it! Each time they catch a strategy or skill in the air, they must move toward doing that each and every time *on their own.* Sometimes we feel like we should jump in and help them. There are definitely times when we do, but there are also times when we must ask, "How can you help yourself?" This is the ultimate question that children must eventually come to ask of themselves.

38

Catch a Falling Reader by . . .

Reflecting on the Way We Do Things

Let me be clear about this: It is never easy to bring about a change of mind.

—Howard Gardner

Good teachers and parents are always evaluating and reevaluating the way they relate to their children. They reflect on what they did and said and what they will do and say. They take time to consider whether they are fostering independence or encouraging dependency. The true test is whether or not our falling readers can become independent and proficient readers, writers, and thinkers.

Take a few minutes to reflect on the way you react and verbally prompt struggling children as you are teaching them to read. Read each item below and circle the response that identifies what you tend to do most often. Then add up all of your A's, B's, C's, and D's. Consult the item analysis at the end of the reflection to check on yourself. I recommend that you do this exercise several times each year to sharpen your saw and to remind yourself to work toward independence at all times.

REFLECTION EXERCISE

1. *When my struggling readers come to words they don't know, I tend to*
   a. Tell them the difficult word when they appear to be stuck
   b. Offer some clues such as the first sound, first syllable, pictures
   c. Give them some wait time, some choices, and maybe tell them the word
   d. Question them about the word they are stuck on

2. *While working with a struggling writer who is having difficulty with spelling, I tend to*
   a. Orally spell a new or difficult word out for them
   b. Write the difficult words down for them to copy
   c. Give them some clues about the first sound, last sound, known chunks, or an analogy to a word they know
   d. Ask them how they could figure out the word on their own.

3. *When struggling readers look up at me and ask for help with a word while reading, I tend to*
   a. Smile and tell them the word.
   b. Give them clues such as the first sound, first syllable, similar rhyming words.
   c. Say "try it" in a supportive voice and then give some clues, if needed
   d. Ask them why they took their eyes off the text

4. *When struggling writers are stuck when writing a new word, I tend to*
   a. Write the word for them so they can move on
   b. Pronounce the word several times loudly
   c. Encourage the children to say the word aloud slowly and then to record what they hear
   d. Ask them what they can do to help themselves

5. *When struggling readers are reading painfully or word by word, I tend to*
   a. Let them finish and praise their efforts
   b. Tell them, "I'll read a page and then you read a page"
   c. Praise them for working so hard, but tell them to read by putting their words together "like we talk." Then read a sentence to model this for them
   d. Ask them why they are reading word by word

6. *When struggling readers are reading and then suddenly look up, off the text, I tend to*
   a. Redirect them with my finger and sometimes tell them the word
   b. Give them some wait time and then tell them the word
   c. Tell them to "keep their eyes on the word" and prompt them with some verbal clues
   d. Ask them why they are looking up on every word that is new or hard

7. *When other students in the group call out a difficult word for falling struggling readers, I tend to*
   a. Encourage the readers to keep reading on
   b. Repeat the correct word for the readers and say "sh" to the others
   c. Tell the other students *not* to call out the words, even though they want to help, and encourage the readers to "try it" alone
   d. Ask the readers why that word is hard when they have seen it so many times before!

8. *When building sight words for falling readers, I tend to*
   a. Use mainly flash cards to teach them these words and often tell them the ones they forget
   b. Refer them to the word wall often
   c. Provide daily practice with reading *and* writing sight words *fast*
   d. Ask them how each sight word is spelled

REFLECTION EXERCISE ITEM ANALYSIS

If you selected

Mostly A's:

You tend to foster dependency and to limit children's ability to problem solve and to use strategies on their own. Stop it!

Mostly B's:

You encourage some independence but still do a lot for the children. This may slow the children's progress.

Mostly C's:

You realize how crucial it is for struggling readers to problem solve and to use a variety of strategies. You use verbal prompts and actions that foster independence in falling readers. Keep it up!

Mostly D's:

You are too concerned with how children process information, and this may be blocking their progress. Focus on helping them internalize the strategies you've been teaching. Stopping to tell you "why" breaks their fluency and comprehension.

39

Catch a
Falling Reader by . . .

Being an Energized Teacher

*All labor that uplifts humanity has dignity and importance
and should be undertaken with painstaking excellence.*

—Martin Luther King Jr.

In his book *On Becoming a Leader*, Warren Bennis (2003) offered a unique comparison between managers and leaders. I can make the same case for tired teachers versus energized teachers. It is my hope that we will all strive to find ways to energize ourselves so that we can make a difference in the lives of every child we teach. Our roles as parents and teachers of children cannot be equaled. Kids know when we are tired, drained, and burned out. They know when we're motivated, happy, and energized. I hope that you will find ways to keep your energy levels high as you catch every single falling reader who crosses your path. As Walt Disney said, "To teach well is also to entertain."

- The tired teacher administers; the energized teacher innovates.
- The tired teacher is a copy; the energized teacher is an original.
- The tired teacher maintains; the energized teacher develops.
- The tired teacher focuses on systems and structure; the energized teacher focuses on children.
- The tired teacher relies on control; the energized teacher inspires trust.
- The tired teacher has a short-range view; the energized teacher has a long-range perspective.
- The tired teacher asks how and when; the energized teacher asks what and why.
- The tired teacher has his or her eye always on the bottom line; the energized teacher has his or her eye on the horizon.
- The tired teacher imitates; the energized teacher originates.
- The tired teacher accepts the status quo; the energized teacher challenges it.
- The tired teacher is the classic good soldier; the energized teacher is his or her own person.
- The tired teacher does things right; the energized teacher does the right thing.

Catch a falling reader, put this falling reader in your pocket, never let one get away.

May the force be with you and your children.

40

Catch a
Falling Reader by . . .

Becoming a
"Starfish Flinger"

I am one, only one. I cannot do everything, but I can do
something. I will not refuse to do the something I can do.

—Helen Keller

At some point, all teachers and parents have asked the following question, "Am I really making a difference?" Too often,
we become discouraged or disillusioned by the sheer numbers of
problems, issues, and casualties that exist for kids in our world. We
wonder if we really are making a difference with the few who
cross our paths. It is my hope that the following story, given to me
by someone who watched me struggle as a novice teacher years
ago, will inspire you as it has me:

THE STARFISH FLINGER

As the old woman walked the beach at dawn, she noticed a young girl ahead of her picking up starfish and flinging them into the sea. Finally catching up with the girl, she asked her why she was doing this. The answer was that the stranded starfish would die if left until the morning sun.

"But the beach goes on for miles and there are millions of starfish," countered the other. "How can your effort make any difference?"

The young girl looked at the starfish in her hand and then threw it to safety in the waves.

"It makes a difference to this one," she said.

—Author Unknown

Become a starfish flinger, for you never know when the falling reader whom you caught today will become a shining star tomorrow. As President Harry Truman once said, "All readers won't become leaders, but all leaders must be readers."

I invite you to join me in my lifelong quest to "Catch Them ALL."

Keep doing great things for kids and literacy!

Write to me with questions or comments. Visit www.conniehebert.com.

Recommended Bibliography, Web Sites, Texts, and Videos

BIBLIOGRAPHY

Armbruster, C. C., Lehr, F., & Osborn, J. (2003). *Put reading first: The research building blocks for teaching children to read* (2nd ed.). Washington, DC: National Institute for Literacy. Retrieved March 7, 2005, from http://www.nifl.gov/nifl/partnershipforreading/publications/PFRbooklet.pdf

Bennis, W. (2003). *On becoming a leader: The leadership classic updated & expanded.* Cambridge, MA: Perseus.

Brown, R., Pressley, M., Van Meter, P., & Schuder, T. (1996). A quasi-experimental validation of transactional strategies instruction with low-achieving second-grade readers. *Journal of Educational Psychology, 88*(1), 18–37.

Carver, R. P., & Liebet, R. E. (1995). The effect of reading library books in different levels of difficulty on gain in reading ability. *Reading Research Quarterly, 30,* 26–48.

Clay, M. M. (1972). *The early detection of reading difficulties.* Auckland, New Zealand: Heinemann.

Clay, M. M. (1993). *An observation survey of early literacy achievement.* Portsmouth, NH: Heinemann.

Dowhower, S. L. (1987). Effects of repeated reading on second-grade transitional readers' fluency and comprehension. *Reading Research Quarterly, 22*(4), 389–404.

Homan, S., Klesius, J. P., & Hite, C. (1993). Effects of repeated readings and non-repetitive strategies on students' fluency and comprehension. *Journal of Educational Research, 87*(2), 94–99.

International Reading Association. (2000). *Excellent reading teachers: A position statement of the International Reading Association.* Barksdale, MD: Author.

International Reading Association. (2000). *Teaching all children to read: The roles of the reading specialist: A position statement of the International Reading Association.* Newark, DE: Author.

Kameenui, E., Carnine, D., & Freschi, R. (1982). Effects of text construction and instructional procedures for teaching word meanings on comprehension and recall. *Reading Research Quarterly, 17*(3), 367–388.

Loranger, A. L. (1997). Comprehension strategies instruction: Does it make a difference? *Reading Psychology, 18*(1), 31–68.

National Reading Panel. (2000). *Teaching children to read: An evidence-based assessment of the scientific research literature on reading and its implications for reading instruction—Reports of the subgroups.* Washington, DC: National Institute of Child Health and Development.

National Research Council. (1999). *Starting out right: A guide to promoting children's reading success.* Washington, DC: National Academy Press.

O'Shea, L. J., Sindelar, P. T., & O'Shea, D. J. (1985). The effects of repeated readings and attentional cues on reading fluency and comprehension. *Journal of Reading Behavior, 17,* 129–142.

Paris, S. G., Saarnio, D. A., & Cross, D. R. (1986). A metacognitive curriculum to promote children's reading and learning. *Australian Journal of Psychology, 38*(2), 107–123.

Pinnell, G. S., Lyons, C. A., DeFord, D. E., Bryk, A. S., & Seltzer, M. (1991). *Studying the effectiveness of early intervention approaches for first grade children having difficulty in reading* (Educational Report No. 16). Columbus: Ohio State University.

Pinnell, G. S., Pikulski, J. J., Wixson, K. K., Campbell, J. R., Gough, P. B., & Beatty, A. S. (1995). *Listening to children reading aloud.* Washington, DC: Office of Educational Research and Improvement, U.S. Department of Education.

Rasinski, T. V. (1990). Effects of repeated reading and listening-while-reading on reading fluency. *Journal of Educational Research, 83*(3), 147–150.

Samuels, S. J. (1976). Automatic decoding and reading comprehension. *Language Arts, 42,* 323–325.

Samuels, S. J. (1997). The method of repeated readings. *The Reading Teacher, 50*(5), 376–381.

Snow, C. E., Burns, M. S., & Griffin, P. (1998). *Preventing reading difficulties in young children.* Washington, DC: National Academy Press.

Stahl, S. A., Jacobson, M. G., & Davis, C. E. (1989). Prior knowledge and difficult vocabulary in the comprehension of unfamiliar text. *Reading Research Quarterly, 24,* 27–43.

Stiggins, R. J. (2001). The principal's leadership role in assessment. *NASSP Bulletin, 85*(621), 13–26.

Stiggins, R. J. (2002). Assessment crisis: The absence of assessment for learning. *Phi Delta Kappan, 758*–765.

Stoddard, K., Valcante, G., Sindelar, P., O'Shea, L., & Algozzine, B. (1993). Increasing reading rate and comprehension: The effects of repeated reading, sentence segmentation, and intonation training. *Reading Research and Instruction, 32,* 53–65.

Wasik, B. A., & Slavin, R. E. (1993). Preventing early reading failure with one-to-one tutoring: A review of five programs. *Reading Research Quarterly, 28,* 179–200.

Wu, H.-M., & Solman, R. T. (1993). Effective use of pictures as extra stimulus prompts. *British Journal of Educational Psychology, 63*(1), 144–160.

WEB SITES

Don Johnston Incorporated. http://www.donjohnston.com (Software for struggling readers).

edHelper. http://www.edhelper.com (For classroom teachers).

Hanson Initiative for Language & Literacy. http://www.mghihp.edu/hill.com?cw=1 (Literacy skill programs).

International Reading Association. http://www.reading.org (For literacy professionals, classroom teachers, special education specialists, and administrators).

Kurzweil Educational Systems. http://www.kurzweiledu.com (Software for dyslexia, ADD, learning disabilities).

READING INSTRUCTION

Bear, D., Invernizzi, M., Templeton, S. R., & Johnston, F. (2007). *Words their way with English learners: Word study for phonics, vocabulary, & spelling instruction* (4th ed.). Upper Saddle River, NJ: Pearson Merrill Prentice Hall.

Byrd, D., & Westfall, P. (2002). *Guided reading coaching tool.* Peterborough, NH: Crystal Springs Books.

Clay, M. (1991). *Becoming literate: The construction of inner control.* Portsmouth, NH: Heinemann.

Cunningham, P. M. (2005). *Phonics they use: Words for reading & writing* (4th ed.). Boston: Pearson/Allyn & Bacon.

Daniels, H. (2001). *Literature circles: Voice & choice in book clubs and reading groups.* Portland, ME: Stenhouse.

Fink, R. (2006). *Why Jane and John couldn't read—and how they learned: A new look at striving readers.* Newark, DE: International Reading Association.

Fountas, I., & Pinnell, G. S. (1999). *Matching books to readers: Using leveled books in guided reading (K–3).* Portsmouth, NH: Heinemann.

Gentry, R. (1999). *The literacy map: Guiding children to where they need to be.* New York: Mondo.

Hebert, C. (2003a). *50 sight-word phrases (1–4).* Peterborough, NH: Crystal Springs Books.

Hebert, C. (2003b). *50 sight-word phrases (PreK–2).* Peterborough, NH: Crystal Springs Books.

Mooney, M. E. (1990). *Reading to, With, and by Children.* Katonah, NY: Richard C. Owen Publishers, Inc.

Opitz, M. F., & Rasinski, T. (1998). *Good-bye round robin: 25 effective oral reading strategies.* Portsmouth, NH: Heinemann.

Opitz, M., & Ford, M. (2001). *Reaching readers: Flexible and innovative strategies for guided reading.* Portsmouth, NH: Heinemann.

Spears, M. (2004). *Shared reading coaching tools.* Peterborough, NH: Crystal Springs Books.

Tovani, C. (2000). *I read it, but I don't get it: Comprehension strategies for adolescent readers.* Portland, ME: Stenhouse.

Trelease, J. (2006). *The read-aloud handbook* (6th ed.). New York: Penguin Books.

WRITING AND COMPREHENSION

Campbell, R. (2001). *Read-alouds with young children.* Newark, DE: International Reading Association.

Clyde, J. A., Barber, S., Hogue, S., & Wasz, L. (2006). *Breakthrough to meaning: Helping your kids become better readers, writers, & thinkers.* Portsmouth, NH: Heinemann.

Dorn, L., & Saffos, C. (2001). *Scaffolding young writers: A writer's workshop approach.* Portland, ME: Stenhouse.

Harvey, S., & Goodvis, A. (2007). *Strategies that work: Teaching comprehension for understanding & engagement.* Portland, ME: Stenhouse.

Miller, D. (2002). *Reading with meaning: Teaching comprehension in the primary grades.* Portland, ME: Stenhouse.

SPECIAL INTEREST

Bracey, G. W. (2006). *Reading educational research: How to avoid getting statistically snookered.* Portsmouth, NH: Heinemann.

Clay, M. (2006). *An observation survey: Survey of early literacy achievement* (Rev. 2nd ed.). Portsmouth, NH: Heinemann.

Covey, S. R. (2005). *The 8th habit: From effectiveness to greatness.* New York: Free Press.

Gardner, H. (2006). *Changing minds: The art & science of changing our own and other people's minds.* Boston: Harvard Business School Press.

Hebert, C. (2006). *Catch a falling teacher.* Philadelphia: Xlibris.

Holliman, L. (1998). *The complete guide to classroom centers.* Huntington Beach, CA: Creative Teaching Press.

Jensen, E. (2005). *Teaching with the brain in mind.* Alexandria, VA: Association for Supervision and Curriculum Development.

Tomlinson, C. A. (2001). *How to differentiate in mixed ability classrooms.* Alexandria, VA: Association for Supervision and Curriculum Development.

Tomlinson, C. A., & McTighe, J. (2006). *Integrating differentiated instruction and understanding by design: Connecting content & kids.* Alexandria, VA: Association for Supervision and Curriculum Development.

Vygotsky, L. S., Cole, M., John-Steiner, V., & Scribner, S. (1978). *Mind in society: Development of higher psychological processes.* Boston: Harvard University Press.

LITERACY VIDEOS FOR USE DURING ON-SITE PROFESSIONAL DEVELOPMENT (ELEMENTARY GRADES)

Dorn, L. (1999). *Organizing for literacy* [Video]. Portland, ME: Stenhouse. (Available from http://www.stenhouse.com/productcart/pc/view Prd.asp?idProduct=312)

Harvey, S., & Goudvis, A. (2002). *Strategy instruction in action* [Video]. Portland, ME: Stenhouse. (Available from http://www.stenhouse. com/productcart/pc/viewPrd.asp?idProduct=335)

Hebert, C. R. (2007). *Catch a model literacy lesson (K–2)* [Video]. West Springfield, MA: Einnoc Educational Enterprises. (Available from http://www.conniehebert.com/products.html)

Index

**CORWIN
PRESS**

The Corwin Press logo—a raven striding across an open book—represents the union of courage and learning. Corwin Press is committed to improving education for all learners by publishing books and other professional development resources for those serving the field of PreK–12 education. By providing practical, hands-on materials, Corwin Press continues to carry out the promise of its motto: **"Helping Educators Do Their Work Better."**